"This book is the heart-wrenching story about a loving wife who grapples with the physical sickness, recovery, and then unexpected death of her husband. It insightfully reveals the emotional rollercoaster she rides, from hope to despair and anger. It demonstrates the adjustments she makes and her personal expectations about the grim realities of life, even among those who confess their faith in Jesus Christ. I trust that this book will help others be encouraged to realize that our God is faithful."

—Rev. Hanford Branscombe

JULIE NOBLE

Transfusion
The Power of the Blood

Scripture taken from the New King James Version®. Copyright © 1982 by Thomas Nelson. Used by permission. All rights reserved. Scriptures taken from the Holy Bible, New International Version®, NIV®. Copyright © 1973, 1978, 1984, 2011 by Biblica, Inc.™ Used by permission of Zondervan. All rights reserved worldwide. www.zondervan.com The "NIV" and "New International Version" are trademarks registered in the United States Patent and Trademark Office by Biblica, Inc.™

ISBN: 978-1-4866-2552-9
eBook ISBN: 978-1-4866-2553-6

Word Alive Press
119 De Baets Street Winnipeg, MB R2J 3R9
www.wordalivepress.ca

WORD ALIVE
—P R E S S—

Cataloguing in Publication information can be obtained from Library and Archives Canada.

Dedication

I dedicate this book to my husband Lloyd, the bravest and most courageous person I know. He had the will to fight and the will to live. Throughout this nightmare, he was my rock and strength. Watching him go through this made me want to be a better person. I love you, Lloyd, with all my heart. My husband and my best friend.

Of course, I also want to thank my wonderful and beautiful daughters whose innocence rocks my world. You are my inspiration. When I look at you, I see peace. Thank you for that. I love you both for being who you are and for being my peacekeepers in times of trouble.

I have just so many other people to thank, including all my friends and family who were there for us financially, emotionally, and mentally. You know who you are and I thank each and every one of you from the bottom of my heart.

A very special thank you goes out to my parents. They were the glue that held us together. I thank you for all your support and prayers and encouragement. Without you, we would not have been able to get through any of this. I love you both so very much.

God has to be given the glory for all this. He was our strength when we were weak. He provided amazing people along the way to help. He covered us and protected us through this journey. He was and always will be in control. He is bigger than any storm imaginable. If trusting God isn't enough, nothing is.

Introduction

This book is written in memory of my husband, Lloyd Lee. In 2001, he was diagnosed with ITP, idiopathic thrombocytopenic purpura, a rare autoimmune disease in which a person's blood doesn't clot properly. I started writing this book when he was alive and it has taken me that long to complete it.

I really want to get out the message that even in the midst of trouble, adversity, chaos, and the storms of life, there is hope and a way to get through them—and that is with the Lord. Some may say that my story didn't have a happy ending because Lloyd passed away, but life doesn't have to end just because a loved one dies; the Lord is our refuge and strength in these times. We have the hope that one day we will be reunited with our loved ones.

I also want to educate people on this horrible disease. When Lloyd was diagnosed, there was barely any knowledge of it, let alone any treatment. If this book helps even one person to have hope, my goal has been met. I'm not doing this to make millions; I just want to help others.

In conclusion, I have a testimony to share about my husband's illness and death—but the story doesn't end there. In fact, my story has only just begun.

One

It's funny how much we take for granted in life. When you're young, especially a stupid, know-it-all teenager, you don't realize how important life is. And you don't realize that it can all be taken away in the blink of an eye.

At a really dark and miserable period of my life, I remember contemplating suicide, thinking I was alone in this world. I didn't think my life was worth living. The older I got, though, the more I've realized that so many others have felt the same way at one point or another. What exactly does a person imagine will happen if they commit suicide? That they will automatically arrive in heaven, coming back from the dead? It's stupid teenager crap, but I sometimes wish I could go back to that instead of living this grown-up adult life of mine with so many responsibilities.

When I was younger, I often had the mindset that nothing bad would ever happen to me, that I was invincible and my actions wouldn't have consequences. The anti-wrinkle creams, the dieting, the cellulite creams, looking twice before crossing the road, scrubbing my hands to make sure all the germs and bacteria are off... now that I'm older, I do everything possible to stay alive as long as I can.

The older you get, the more you wish your life would slow down. But when you're young, you can't wait to grow up and be an adult and live independently.

Well, I thank God that I never followed through with my thoughts of suicide. If I had, I never would have had the honour of marrying my wonderful husband and being a mother to my two beautiful and perfect daughters. And I wouldn't have been able to share my story, the one that changed my life forever.

It started four years ago, in March 2001. I was eight months pregnant with my first child, Delaney. We were very excited, as most first-time parents would be. We couldn't wait to see her enter the world. That said, at times I didn't want to give birth. At least when she was in my stomach, I could protect her. Little did I know that I would have to do exactly that in the very first minute of her life!

During the pregnancy, my husband woke up one morning with a weird-looking rash all over his body. He was covered in bruises. His parents and sister were visiting for the week, as it was March break. We lived in Ottawa and his family lived in Oshawa.

"Julie, you have to stop beating me up," he jokingly said.

His mother, a nurse, turned to him with a much concerned look. "You should really get that looked at. It looks like it could be a problem with your platelets."

What the heck were platelets?

His dad, sister, and I brought him to our family doctor, who sent Lloyd up to the hospital right away. He didn't like what he saw.

Being eight months pregnant, with all the raging hormones that come with that, I freaked out and started to hyperventilate, obviously thinking the worst. Hoping for the best but thinking the worst.

When we got to the hospital, Lloyd's dad and sister sat in the emergency waiting room while I went back with him. Right away, the staff conducted a ton of bloodwork. It seemed like forever before we saw a doctor!

Lloyd was lying on the bed behind a curtain when the emergency doctor came in and told us that he had paged an oncologist who would arrive shortly. What the heck was an oncologist?

Finally, the oncologist came in. I had a feeling I wasn't going to like him or what he had to say.

My suspicions were right; I didn't like him or what he was going to say. He told Lloyd that he had a platelet count of zero. The normal range for platelets in a man is 150,000 to 450,000 per microliter of blood. All the rest of his bloodwork was off, too. His white blood count was up.

"Platelets clot your blood when you bleed," the doctor explained. "If you cut yourself, it's the platelets that stop the bleeding."

And he had none. Zero!

This all meant that Lloyd was bleeding internally, which explained the bruising all over his body. The weird-looking rash was called petechiae—in other words, blood blisters underneath the skin.

According to the oncologist, there could be two possible causes: an autoimmune disease called ITP or leukaemia.

Right away, my mouth dropped to the floor. Oh my God! Cancer?

Lloyd would have to stay and have a few more tests done. He would also need more monitoring.

"I don't understand why he can't come home with me now," I said. "We could come back tomorrow for more tests. I just want my husband home."

I will never forget the doctor's gut-wrenching next words: "Do you want your husband to die? Because that is what will happen if he goes home right now."

At that point, I went out to the waiting room to explain what was going on to Lloyd's dad and sister. When they went back to see him, I proceeded to find a payphone to call my own mom and dad. They also lived in Oshawa, which seemed like a million miles away. I called them collect and told them what was going on, that we were at the emergency room with Lloyd and the doctors didn't know what was wrong with him.

I lost it completely. It's a miracle my daughter wasn't born prematurely.

My parents packed up and came to Ottawa the next day.

Over the next few weeks, Lloyd underwent lots of bloodwork and saw a haematologist who gave him some very intense IV treatments called IVIG (intravenous immunoglobulin) to protect his remaining platelets from being eaten away any further. The doctors also put him on a high dose of prednisone steroids and gave him platelet transfusions.

Soon they were able to determine that he did have ITP (idiopathic thrombocytopenic purpura), not leukaemia. This is a rare blood disease. Something in his body was attacking his platelets for some unknown reason. The doctors also thought it would be best to remove his spleen, as there was a fifty-fifty chance that his spleen was eating his platelets. They described it to us like a game of Pacman.

The big question was, would we have him go through surgery now, before the baby was born? Or would we wait until after the birth, so at least he could be present in the delivery room and move around and hold his newborn?

Together with the haematologist, Lloyd and I decided to wait.

Delaney was born five days late. I had laboured all day at home alongside my mom, who had been staying with us for the last two weeks. Lloyd had just gotten back from a treatment of IVIG at the hospital, but at 5:00 p.m. we got a call from the staff informing us that Lloyd needed to come back in. The current treatments just weren't doing the trick.

We went in together. When we got to the room in the emergency department, I lay down in his bed since my contractions were getting more intense and painful. But I didn't want to leave him.

Meanwhile, my mom had been calling everybody in the family. Now my dad was on the way, along with my sister, my niece and nephew, and Lloyd's mother and sister. We were going to have a full house in that hospital when Delaney arrived!

My labour soon got so bad that the nurses demanded I go down to the delivery room. My mom walked me down and helped get me all set up. Once she saw I was in good hands, she walked back across the hospital to be with Lloyd.

The birth of our first baby was a very emotional time for both of us, with Lloyd being sick and needing all these treatments!

After fighting with the doctor for several minutes, he finally decided to let Lloyd come down to the delivery room to be with me. No way was he going to miss the birth of his firstborn. He just had to sign a waiver stating that if anything happened to him while going back and forth, the hospital wasn't liable.

So they hooked him up to another round of IVIG and my mom wheeled him down to the delivery room. After one treatment was over, my mom would push him back to the emergency department and get him hooked up to the second. It continued in this vein, with each treatment lasting an hour and a half. Thank God for my mother! It's true what they say; you never stop needing them, no matter the situation or how old you get.

Lloyd finally finished his treatments around 11:00, but there was still no baby. Little did we know that we would have a bit of a wait!

Delaney was finally born the next morning, at 8:01 on Wednesday, April 18, 2001. It was the happiest day of our lives. We were both so exhausted and couldn't wait for things to settle down.

But they didn't, not for a while. Lloyd was able to stay in the hospital with me on a cot for the two days I spent there. The staff bent the rules because of his situation and allowed him to stay. This made me happy, since I could keep an eye on him, too. The three of us could bond as a family.

When we got home, you would think it would be a relief for us to finally get some peace and quiet. Well, that didn't happen either. Lloyd got a phone call from the hospital on account of some new bloodwork he had done while at the hospital. His platelet count was still quite low. Dangerously low, in fact. The doctors wanted to admit him for a few days.

Real nice, I thought. On the third day of our baby's life, and our first day home, he had to go back to the hospital! What was I going to do? I didn't know how to look after a baby by myself, nor did I want to do this alone. This was so unfair. What had we done to deserve this?

My in-laws decided to stay. But even though they were present, I never felt so alone. Delaney was only three days old and I felt like a bad mother because I didn't know what to do or how to do it. I felt like a bad wife, too, because I couldn't do anything to help my husband. It's beyond my understanding how I got through these times without going insane.

Two

The doctors decided to perform Lloyd's splenectomy in May. Delaney was about a month old and Lloyd would have to be off work for at least a month with recovery. It was the first time he took any amount of time off, since throughout this whole ordeal he had managed to keep going to work between treatments. I don't think either of us realized at the time how severe his condition was.

He made it through surgery with flying colours, although of course he was very sore and in quite a bit of pain. He bore an everlasting scar on his stomach where the doctors took his spleen, a daily reminder to us of how sick he was.

Of course, we were told that we wouldn't know the outcome for quite a while. So we waited patiently. Lloyd got bloodwork taken on a regular basis to make sure his platelet counts weren't dropping. So far so good. After surgery, he was on quite a high dose of prednisone, which helped.

There we were at home with a new baby and a sick father. He couldn't even hold Delaney for the longest time, but he finally got his strength up and was able to enjoy her like a father should.

What an emotional rollercoaster this was! It all happened within three months. My whole world was shaken.

If it was that bad for me, imagine what it was like for Lloyd. But did he complain, even once? No, he didn't. I think he was more concerned with me, especially when I was pregnant and we first brought Delaney home from the hospital. He worried about my sanity and my concern for him. Everything had happened so fast that we didn't have a lot of time to get depressed; we had to make fast decisions.

Soon it seemed like the nightmare was behind us. Lloyd got regular checkups and we went on with our lives, thanking God every step of the way for having healed Lloyd of this whole ITP problem. I have to give God a lot of the credit for getting us through. I do believe He was watching over us. I had faith that Lloyd would get better.

Two years passed and a lot of changes occurred. We sold our house in Ottawa and moved back to Oshawa to be with family. I also got pregnant with our second child, another girl. Lloyd didn't have to go in for checkups anymore. Life was hectic, but it was a good hectic. He started a new job in Toronto and I stayed home, enjoying Delaney and my pregnancy.

I gave birth to Ella on Friday, January 17, 2003 at 11:15 p.m. The delivery went well, but it was fast. The memories of my last delivery were still quite clear, but this one was much better. It was a happier experience because we were able to concentrate fully on Ella.

Then, two months later, something happened one night that I remember quite well.

Lloyd's parents were over and had brought friends of theirs to see our house. In the middle of this, Lloyd took me upstairs and showed me some bruising on his legs. He then called his mom up to look at it, because he didn't want everyone to know. She didn't have much to say except that he should go see the doctor.

"It's probably nothing, but get it checked anyway," she said.

I think she knew that something wasn't right, but she didn't want to scare us.

When our company left, Lloyd got on the internet and did some research. Of course, all the results suggested leukaemia.

We specifically remembered that first night at the hospital, when the doctors had given us two possible diagnoses: ITP or leukaemia.

Lloyd and I started to cry right away. We thought his ITP had been cured, leaving only one possibility. How could he have leukemia? This wasn't right. He was twenty-nine years old.

He went to the doctor the next day and was once again sent to the hospital and referred to a haematologist.

Here we go again, I remember thinking.

When he got the bloodwork done, lo and behold, his platelets were low. Lloyd explained his history to the haematologist and was told that once you have ITP, you are never cured. The specialist was pretty sure this wasn't leukaemia. No, it was a relapse of ITP, after two years of remission.

None of our previous doctors in Ottawa had explained to us that ITP would never go away, that this was an autoimmune disease he would have for the rest of his life.

So once again Lloyd was put on prednisone and had to come in for treatments of IVIG.

We weren't quite sure if this was going to affect his job. Nobody wanted a "sick" person at work, especially someone who might have to take time off for treatments. But amazingly his boss was very receptive on hearing about his story and seemed to be understanding. He didn't need time off right away, but we didn't know what the future would hold.

We were grateful for the fact that this time Lloyd's condition didn't seem to be so serious. We were also grateful to the doctors for giving him the right treatments, which seemed to work well and act fast.

From March to November, everything was fine. Lloyd went in for regular bloodwork and checkups. His haematologist watched him closely. Lloyd felt fine.

Every year during November, Lloyd liked to go hunting. He went away up north with my dad, cousins, and uncle and had a great time. It was good for him, like a reward for the year. He worked so hard and really didn't ask for much. He never complained about anything. So this was the one time of year he could get away and do something for himself.

Yup, you guessed it, on this year's hunting trip he suffered a drop in platelets again. The year before, he hadn't been able to go on account of moving and starting a new job. This year, he had been especially excited about the trip.

It seemed like Lloyd could always predict when his platelets were low, due to certain symptoms. In addition to the obvious bruising and petechiae, he would feel really tired, have low energy, and get very cold.

What irked me most about this relapse is that he had known his platelets were low but still went hunting. Typical man.

He finally went to his haematologist and got bloodwork done. Sure enough, his platelets were, in fact, low. Poor Lloyd would have to miss out on another year of hunting.

I was starting to believe he just wasn't meant to go.

Lloyd was more ticked off about not being able to go hunting than the fact that his platelets were low and he needed to go through more treatments.

This time, it seemed like they were a bit harder to get under control. His haematologist recommended that he take time off work until this got settled, so for the second time in three years Lloyd went on short-term disability.

Great… right around Christmas. Thank God the kids were so little that they wouldn't notice, or really even care about, the lack of gifts under the tree. It was depressing, though, because Christmas was a family occasion—and we couldn't buy gifts for our family.

So there we were during the holiday season, with no money, no gifts, and feeling sorry for ourselves, I guess you could say. At least Lloyd was alive and these treatments seemed to be working. Slowly, sure, but nonetheless working.

On New Year's Eve, we sat alone, again feeling sorry for ourselves because we couldn't go out or spend any money. We didn't realize at the time that things could have been a lot worse.

Little did I know that they would get much worse down the road. If I knew then what I know now, I would have slapped us both across the face and said, "Let's get on with it! What good is it to sit around and feel sorry for ourselves?" We didn't have any money, but at least we had each other.

What about the simple things in life, like enjoying a cup of coffee or laughing at a funny movie or sitting down with a good book? Do people do that anymore? Or are people too busy to enjoy the simple things? I was one of those people. A busy mom of two small and very active kids. I couldn't remember the last time I'd actually sat down and enjoyed my cup of coffee. Sat down and actually tasted and savoured each sip. I loved my coffee and had it every morning, but I always drank it in intervals, between giving the kids breakfast, running downstairs to put a load of laundry in, and feeding the dog.

I had to learn to take time for my coffee, as simple as that is. I'm taking the time now. Life is so short and it can be taken away in a second.

Three

Lloyd got better, as I knew he would, and went back to work in the new year. He still had to go into the hospital for regular bloodwork and checkups, even though he felt good. But I constantly asked him, "Are you feeling okay? Are your platelets low?" He always gave me a chuckle and said, "I'm fine, Julie. You're paranoid."

Maybe he was right. Maybe I was just a little bit paranoid. Maybe I was even a little bit obsessed. I think any wife in my position would have been. I loved my husband and wanted to make sure he was okay. Obviously, going by that little hunting episode in November, I couldn't trust him to tell me everything. I had to ask.

I wish that was the end of my story, but unfortunately it was just the beginning.

The rest of the year was great and Lloyd actually got to go hunting for the first time in two years the next fall. He felt good and was so happy to get away for a week. The kids and I, along with my mom, even went up to the hunting camp for the weekend. Everything was normal and right, the way it should have been.

Christmas, too, was very nice. We made up for the year before. Then we planned to travel to Ottawa for New Year's and spend it with some old friends. Lloyd had a follow-up appointment scheduled for December 29 but had no symptoms of a relapse. We figured everything was fine. And why would we think any different?

He called me from the hospital that day and reported the bad news: his platelets were low. I thought he was joking and didn't believe him at first, but it was true. His platelets had dropped to 40,000. His doctor had sent him home and told him to stay close over the next few days and come back in a week for another checkup.

As you can well imagine, we were down in the dumps and depressed, especially Lloyd. I started to unpack our stuff. We called everyone we needed to call and proceeded to sit home alone for New Year's Eve. Which was okay. At least it was nice and quiet.

This was kind of like the calm before the storm.

He went back to work in the new year and did more bloodwork the next Wednesday. His platelets were still pretty low, but the doctor just told him to come back in a week's time.

So that's what he did. The following Wednesday, he went back again. The result? Low platelets.

Now the doctor decided to try the same treatment that had previously been effective. It was time for more IVIG.

The routine went as follows: he would go in for bloodwork to get his platelet count before treatment, then leave the office and walk around the corner to the chemo area. He had to sit in an easy chair and be hooked up to the IV there, just like all the other people receiving chemo for cancer. He felt for the longest time that he shouldn't have been there because he didn't have cancer. He would look around and observe all the people who were worse off than him.

That was the thing with Lloyd; he could find the best in every bad situation. He didn't feel sorry for himself. As for the cancer patients, they varied from the really young, like him, to the elderly.

Lloyd started going in for his treatments before work, but he found this hard because the process made him tired. He still went every day.

Finally, after a few days, he changed his routine and started going for treatment on his way home from work instead.

This man was the most amazing person I'd ever met. He was sick—very sick, in fact, and didn't really know it—but he still went into work. Unbelievable!

After three weeks of IVIG treatments, his platelets weren't rising. Either they stayed the same or even went down. We couldn't wrap our heads around what was happening. The doctor even told him that he couldn't go to work anymore until his platelets went up and stabilized for a while. He wrote a doctor's note, which meant going back on short-term disability. Okay. That was no big deal. He'd been on it before and it hadn't lasted very long. That was his mindset anyway, trying to make the best of a bad situation.

Lloyd needed to continue coming in for IVIG treatments, according to the doctor, since that was the most effective way to boost platelet production. So he continued going in. I was fortunate enough to go with him sometimes. I would drop the kids off with my parents, wanting to be there to keep him company. The treatments took anywhere from one to three hours, depending on his vitals. Sometimes he developed high blood pressure and the nurses would have to slow things down.

It was also a very depressing place to be. The room smelled of cancer. Everywhere you looked, you were looking at someone with no hair or someone being sick because they couldn't tolerate the chemo or someone sleeping because the chemo had knocked them out. Every once in a while, I would have to leave and take a walk outside for a couple of minutes just to get a grip on things. None of this was making sense. Why was all this happening?

The doctor decided to run more tests on Lloyd to see whether his spleen had grown back, which was a very small possibility. There could have been a small piece of root left over from the splenectomy years ago.

For this, he had to undergo three different tests.

The first was a denatured red blood cell test. They took some of his blood, heated it up, and administered it back into his system. That would show any sign of a spleen. This test came back negative.

The second test was a spleen scan, which also came back negative. We had really been hoping and praying that a spleen had grown back. That would have explained everything.

The third test was a full body scan, which also came back negative.

After another week or so of this treatment, there was still no improvement. We were very frustrated.

It was becoming normal for me to go with him for treatments every day. My parents were awesome about taking the kids, because they kind of knew the feeling of wanting to sit with somebody during treatment. They had done that when my grandmother was dying of cancer and needed extensive chemo.

I will never forget what the doctor said to us next. Before Lloyd's treatment one day, with still no improvement, he gave us the option of actually trying chemo. He had to be kidding! Chemo? Lloyd didn't have cancer. So why would the doctor suggest that?

"Chemo is a very strong and powerful way to kill off your cells and antibodies," the doctor explained. "In Lloyd's case, that's what is causing the problem. If you kill off antibodies, your system can produce new ones. Hopefully good ones."

But first he agreed to try Lloyd on a few more treatments of IVIG before making a recommendation.

It was time for Lloyd to go into the treatment room. Since I could hardly contain myself, I told him that I needed to use the bathroom and would be right back.

My God, I prayed, worrying I was about to pass out. *Help him, God!*

I walked out to the payphones, called my parents, and told them about what the doctor had told us. I don't remember what I said. All I remember is crying so hard that I could barely speak.

This was bad now. Really bad. For some reason, I associated chemo with cancer and how bad cancer was.

After I got myself together, I went back in and sat with Lloyd. He was quiet and knew I had been crying. I never wanted to cry in front of him.

My thirty-year-old husband needed to have chemo. I'd heard about such things all the time, but you never guess it's going to happen to you.

I don't think Lloyd and I said much to each other for the rest of the time we were at the hospital that day. Neither one of us really had to say anything. We knew what was on each other's minds.

After we left the hospital, the second hardest thing we had to do that day was explain to his parents what was going on. He didn't want to tell them on the phone, so we stopped by their house on the way home from the hospital.

As soon as we walked in their house, they both knew and sensed that something was wrong. I'll never forget it. As soon as Lloyd told his mother, she left the room. A couple of minutes later, his dad went after her. She went upstairs to her room. Like me, she didn't want to cry in front of Lloyd.

Lloyd and I were left to just stare at each other across the table. Both of us had tears in our eyes.

A few days passed and the doctor decided that he didn't want to wait anymore, so Lloyd started a very potent dose of chemo in pill form. These pills are very poisonous, so we had to make sure they were kept in a lockbox. The pills were called cyclophosphamide and Lloyd had to make sure to drink lots of water while on them.

After a couple of weeks, and still showing no improvement, the doctor wasn't happy. Lloyd hadn't responded at all. It would normally take four to six weeks to see any result, but the doctor didn't want to wait that long. So he added another chemo pill, this one called danazol.

The weekend of the Super Bowl was a very big deal to Lloyd and my family. My dad always held a gameday party, with Lloyd attending with my cousins and uncles.

The night before, we were having Lloyd's parents over for supper and Lloyd looked really pale. Something just wasn't right. He knew his platelets were low, but he didn't realize just how low.

He went to the bathroom and right away came out and said a couple of choice words.

"What's wrong?" I asked, even though I knew. There was blood in his urine. I knew it because that would be the next thing to happen. The doctor had warned us about this and said that we needed to go straight to the hospital if it happened.

So off we went, with Lloyd's parents staying with the kids.

When a person's platelets are low, their immune system is no good, which means they can get very sick after being exposed to colds or flus. Well, as soon as we walked into the emergency department, we explained his condition and right away they placed him in a back room away from the rest of the patients.

We waited and waited. It seemed like all we did that night was sit and wait. A couple of different nurses came to take his blood, since it was so hard to find a vein. The doctor, afraid of a brain haemorrhage, contacted the on-call haematologist, who in turn advised the hospital to admit him.

This was total déjà vu. All the memories from Ottawa were coming back to me.

Lloyd kept telling me to go home, but I wasn't going to leave him there. I didn't want to ever leave him. I wasn't going anywhere until he was settled into his room and I knew what they were going to do to help him.

Finally, they got his blood results back. His platelets were down to 7. Not 7,000, not 700… but 7. Deathly low.

I was now afraid he would die in his sleep from internal bleeding or bump his head. I didn't want him going to sleep, even though I knew the rest and sleep would be good for him.

The nurses took him up to his room on the isolation floor. I followed them up and helped answer the nurse's questions. She told me I could stay as long as I wanted.

The staff were wonderful there and assured me they would check on him every hour to get his vitals. That gave me a little bit of comfort. At least if I couldn't be there, someone else would.

I decided to go home, since Lloyd's parents were probably exhausted and worried. I gave him a goodnight kiss and walked out to my car, crying the whole way.

I remember this night as though it were yesterday. The sky was so dark and I could barely see the road through the impenetrable fog and my tears. I do believe in angels, because that's the only way I got home safe and sound that night.

By the time I crawled into bed, I was thoroughly worn out. I felt so sad, so alone, and so scared. I went into Delaney's room, carried her into my bed, and cuddled her all night. I couldn't bear to sleep alone.

When I awoke the next morning, I had to put on my brave face and explain to my two children why Daddy wasn't home and why I had to drop them off at Nani and Pop's house for the day. It wasn't easy trying to explain to Delaney why she couldn't come to the hospital to see Daddy. It broke my heart. Delaney was only four and Ella two; they didn't understand what was going on. They just knew Daddy wasn't home.

As hard as it was, I held back my tears and continued on with the morning. I called all our friends and family who didn't yet know what had happened, telling the whole painful story over and over. Some very dear friends said that they were going to come down from Toronto to see Lloyd and spend some time in the hospital with him.

Oh yeah, it was now Super Bowl Sunday! Of all the days to be in the hospital…

After I dropped the kids off at my parents, I headed back to the hospital, again crying the whole way there. I had to get it out of my system before I saw Lloyd.

When I got there, he seemed to be in pretty good spirits. The only thing he complained about was how he was going to watch the Super Bowl on the tiny TV in his room. I spent the day with him, and he had a few visitors as well. His parents and sister brought lunch and stayed a while.

Then our pastor from church showed up. I was so happy to see him! He sat and prayed with us and for Lloyd. He placed his hands upon Lloyd and cried with us.

I think by now people were really starting to feel that this problem wasn't under control, and it wasn't going away. We were all realizing how scary the situation was.

The doctors were now giving Lloyd actual platelet transfusions. He was also getting a high dose of steroids through IV. It seemed like the staff came and took blood from him every hour, but the results were always the same. The platelets were low and not coming up.

Our friends from Toronto arrived. God bless them, they actually stayed and watched the Super Bowl with Lloyd so he wouldn't be alone. When they showed up, I decided that it was time for me to leave and get my kids. So I gave Lloyd a kiss and went out to the car, once again crying the whole way.

My whole family was at my parents' house for the Super Bowl. I know I should have put on a brave face when I walked in the door, but this time I couldn't. I was too tired of being brave and strong.

I can still feel the presence of an angel right beside me, and of course the presence of the Lord. At this point I was learning to lean on God more and more to help me through.

Four

You know how in life there are certain people who just know your pain and what you're going through without you having to say a word? Well, I have one of those people in my life.

When I walked into my parents' house, my mom greeted me at the door and hugged me.

But then my cousin walked into the room and just looked at me. I went right over to him, he held me, and we both cried. My sweet cousin knew my pain. He who has always been like an older brother to me didn't say a word. That's something you just need sometimes, not to necessarily talk about it but just be held and be given the permission to cry and let it all out. He gave me that. Being in his arms, I knew that I didn't have to be brave, at least not right then and there. Thank God for my wonderful cousin/big brother.

What he said to me after that hit me like a ton of bricks. We talked about Lloyd and the ineffective treatments, and then he brought up the idea of going to the U.S. for treatment. We talked about the possibility of selling our house if we had to and going anywhere in the world if it would help save Lloyd's life.

At first, I thought there was no way I could mention this to Lloyd. He was going to think I was crazy. He wouldn't want to travel anywhere.

But the more my cousin and I talked, the more it made sense to me. I thought to myself, *Forget this. I don't care what Lloyd says. I'm going to do as much research as possible and go to China if we have to.*

For the next couple of days, I did some research on the internet, not knowing where to even look. I persevered.

When I picked Lloyd up at the hospital on Monday, he was being discharged. Big surprise: his platelets were up to 10. After all those treatments and IVs, there hadn't been much improvement from his admission on Saturday.

He would have to go to a follow-up with his haematologist at the Oshawa hospital on Wednesday, though. We were told to give the treatments a couple more days to settle into Lloyd's system before he got more bloodwork done. That way, they would really be able to tell whether the treatments had worked.

On Wednesday, we dropped the kids off at my parents' house and went to his follow-up appointment. After the bloodwork, we sat in the waiting room until his name was called.

Finally, we were called back to see his doctor. We knew by the look on the nurse's face that it wasn't good news. His platelets had dropped to something like 7 again. As we sat waiting, we both cried. What was happening? After all these treatments and time, nothing was helping. Our frustration was moving towards anger.

His doctor came in, sat down, and looked us straight in the eyes. "None of these treatments are working and I'm running out of options. Go home and spend your last days with your family. There's nothing more I can do for you."

I'm sorry, what? I thought. *Are you kidding me? You're his doctor! You don't have the option to just say, "There's nothing more I can do." You're not allowed to say that.*

Frankly, this was unacceptable.

I saw the desperation on my husband's face and decided to keep fighting. I asked whether there were any treatments in the U.S. Lloyd had been doing some research on ITP and had seen something about a life-saving drug called Rituxan. It was used to treat people with ITP and had been successful for some. The only problem was that it was still in the experimental stage and was offered only in the U.S.

"It's very expensive and not a hundred percent guaranteed," the doctor said. "But if you're willing to travel, I would suggest going to the Mayo Clinic in Rochester, Minnesota."

We decided that this is what we would do, but our doctor couldn't be a part of the planning process because of the because of OHIP (Ontario Health Insurance Plan). So we would have to do it on our own. And although there would be no funding, the hospital would contact a social worker to help us with the airline tickets and travel.

One step at a time.

We were still processing the doctor's words—"There's nothing more I can do for you"—when Lloyd was sent back to the treatment room. These additional treatments had already been booked for the day.

The nurses were unbelievably supportive and cried with us as they led us to a private room in the back. They also printed off some flight information and a map that showed us exactly where the Mayo Clinic was situated.

Never in a million years had I ever thought I would face the possibility of losing my husband, especially this way. All I knew was that I had to fight, fight, fight and never give up until I got answers—until he was better.

I knew right then and there that I had to be strong and be the rock for both of us.

That didn't mean I couldn't have moments when I cried, because I did plenty of that. It just meant I couldn't cry in front of Lloyd and show him my fear.

Throughout this day, I learned how important it was to pray. I had grown up always knowing God and believing in Him and the power of prayer. But this was different. I really got up close and personal with Him now and learned how to pray and trust. I depended upon that power of prayer and took personal time with God whenever I could get it.

To be honest, the rest of my day kind of seemed like a blur. I don't really remember much more except that we once again left the hospital and stopped in at Lloyd's parents' house to let them know in person what was going on. As you can well imagine, they didn't take it very well. We then headed over to my parents' house to pick up the kids and fill them in on the latest.

When we got home, I think all we did for the first couple of hours was sit, hold our kids, and cry. Delaney and Ella knew something was wrong, especially Delaney.

I remember lying in bed that night just talking and holding each other. Lloyd wanted to talk about death, but I kept trying to change the subject because I didn't want to face that—and I knew it was hard for him to talk about. He was scared he would die, as was I, but I put it far out of my mind. I had to! I couldn't think about that possibility. I wasn't going to give up.

The next day, Lloyd got another treatment in the hospital, getting topped up with actual platelets. My morning was spent calling the Mayo Clinic and trying to find someone to talk to who would understand.

The first time I called, I got a really nice woman. I don't know if she was a switchboard operator or a receptionist in a doctor's office, but she was very helpful and gave me the number to the haematology department.

I called that department and got another very nice woman. I explained my situation.

"I can put you in for next Tuesday," she said.

"You know what?" I replied. "That's probably a very good response time, but I can't afford to wait. My husband is going to die. I need him to see a doctor now."

She took down my name and number and assured me that either she or the haematologist would call me back.

Great, I thought. *Nobody's taking me seriously. I'm going to give it an hour and then call back if I don't hear anything.*

Within ten minutes, the phone rang. I couldn't believe that it was a haematologist on the other end, returning my call. I explained to him what had been happening with Lloyd since New Year's and told him what our doctor had said.

"Are you able to help?" I asked.

We talked about the option of administering Rituxan. He told me that if we were able to travel, he could help us. That was music to my ears. All we needed to do was be at the Mayo Clinic the following morning at 10:00.

"Thank you," I said as he gave me all the information I'd need. "Thank you very much."

When I got off the phone, I once again sat and cried. I cried because I was scared, I cried because I was happy someone was finally going to do something, and I cried because I was so overwhelmed.

Lloyd called from the hospital shortly after that and I told him everything. The nurses then got in touch with a social worker at the hospital who arranged the flights.

Shortly after these plans were made, Lloyd's sister came over to see me on her way to work. I told her what had just happened and we both cried. One thing about her is that even though she's much younger than me, I see her as a strong person who isn't as emotional as me, which can sometimes be a good thing.

I really wanted her to come with us. I was having all these feelings of loneliness and fear and I needed to be there for Lloyd. But who was going to be there for me?

She didn't stay long, but when she was leaving we just stood in the hallway and hugged each other.

"I wish I could go with you," she cried.

"Me too."

When she left, I thought about her actually coming with us. Why couldn't she? So it would mean getting an extra plane ticket. So what? In the grand scheme of things, who cared about money when we were trying to save Lloyd's life?

Soon after she left, Lloyd's mom called, having heard what was going on. Without hesitation, his parents got in touch with a travel agent and ordered an extra plane ticket. Thank God! I was so grateful. I was relieved that I wouldn't have to do this by myself. I didn't even talk it over with Lloyd first. It was just a snap decision and I didn't care whether he would be mad.

I then called my cousin's wife and asked her to come over, since I didn't want to be alone. She dropped everything and came. I don't know how I appeared to her, but I felt overwhelmed and scatterbrained.

She sat with me in my bedroom as I started to pack our clothes. It was so hard and I didn't know where to start, how much to pack, or for how many days. She was great. She entertained the kids, too.

I thank God every day that our girls were so small and young that they won't remember any of this.

My cousin's wife was just as overwhelmed as I was, but she stayed with me as long as she could. Before she left, my neighbour came over and the three of us sat in my kitchen. I don't remember being very emotional during our talk. I think I was so overwhelmed that I didn't have time to actually think about what was happening. It felt more like a dream.

Afterward my mom and dad picked up Lloyd from the hospital. A few people came over to the house, including my aunt and uncle and the pastor and his wife. We all stood in a circle, with Lloyd in the middle holding our girls' hands. We all laid our hands on him and the pastor began to pray. Everyone was crying, even my dad. I've only ever seen my dad cry a few times; when I saw him crying, I knew he was scared and feeling just as overwhelmed as I was.

When the pastor finished the prayer, we all gathered around in a group hug, knowing and believing that God was going to carry us through and take care of Lloyd.

Everyone but my parents left. The four of us just sat down and I remember being kind of speechless.

My neighbour had given me a card earlier, and I had just put it aside. I opened it now in front of my parents and Lloyd. Inside was some American money. Lloyd's parents, too, had delivered a very generous cheque from his family doctor. We were completely stunned at this generosity.

Later that evening, Lloyd received many phone calls from family and friends wishing him well, including his aunt and uncle, who cried, unable to believe how bad things were. My cousin came over with a card, inside of which was still more American money. My own aunt and uncle did the same. All this kindness overwhelmed me.

We ended up having enough money to live on while staying at the Mayo Clinic. My parents also put money on our credit card to make sure we had enough. And we did! We didn't go without, not even once.

During this time, my sister called every day to check on us and pray with me. I would call her too, as my voice of reason. We ended each conversation in prayer.

The day I made all the arrangements to go to the Mayo Clinic, I called her at work and just lost it. Even though she was at work, she let me cry. I could even sense the fear and pain in her voice. I know she wanted to be with us so bad but couldn't. I also knew she was with me and Lloyd in heart. She and my brother-in-law would never stop praying.

Five

We put the kids to bed and then went to bed once everyone had left. I don't think either of us slept all night. I guess it was around 10:00 p.m. when we went to bed. We just lay there and cried and held each other.

I felt so guilty about leaving the kids and was going to miss them so much. I even crept into Delaney's room at some point in the night and slept with her for a while. Well, I didn't sleep; I cried as I held her. Then I did the same with Ella, just holding on to her as tight as I could.

Our wakeup time, 3:00 a.m., came extremely fast. My parents were the first to arrive that morning to see us off and stay with the kids. My mom and I hugged each other and cried. Now I was emotional. It was very scary, and we were all thinking the exact same thing. Was Lloyd going to come home? Or was I coming home without a husband? I had never in my life seen anybody look so sick—and I had seen a lot of sick people, people dying of cancer. Lloyd looked worse than that. He was pale, with bruises and petechiae all over his body.

We were faced with some travel problems related to his health. His platelets were still extremely low, since the treatments hadn't taken. You would think having had actual platelet transfusions would help somewhat, but no. The nurses at the hospital had also told him that he was at higher risk of having a heart attack or stroke while flying. Was he even going to survive the plane ride? I just put my trust and faith in God. That's all I could do. Everything was so far out of my control.

Right before we left, Lloyd and I went upstairs to peek at the girls one last time. We were both crying and Lloyd was really trembling. Then his parents and sister came to pick us up and we all hugged each other.

As we left, I had never been so scared in my whole life. I couldn't believe this was happening. I didn't want to believe it was happening. I didn't want to leave my girls, I didn't want to leave my house, and I didn't want to leave my parents and my family. The whole way to the airport, I prayed silently.

We got there in good time and checked in. Then it was time to go our separate ways from Lloyd's parents. Lloyd's mom hugged me and I will never forget the words she whispered in my ears: "Get him better and bring him home."

"I will," I said. What else could I say? I wasn't even sure he would get better.

We went through security and customs. We still had about an hour before boarding the plane, so we got coffee and had something to eat even though we weren't really hungry.

Now that we were sitting at the airport and had some time to think, I started to get nauseous. I had flown only once in my life and had sworn never to do it again. I started to freak out and hyperventilate. According to Lloyd and his sister, I gave them a good comedy show for a while. Personally I didn't see what was so funny, but they did! I got no support from them; they were master fliers and didn't see the big deal. I guess it was good for them to laugh and break the tension a bit.

I was shaking uncontrollably when the time came to board the plane. Luckily we had gotten three seats together and I sat in the middle. I wanted nothing to do with sitting by the window!

During takeoff, I thought I was going to vomit all over. I held both of their hands and closed my eyes. I even cried a little. And to make matters worse, we didn't have a direct flight. We had to switch planes in Detroit and do it all over again. More time to get nauseous! Plus, I got searched at a security gate in Detroit. I was the only one out of the three of us.

You would think the second time around would be easier, but it was actually worse. Lloyd and his sister laughed again, which was fine under the circumstances. This plane was even smaller than the last, if that was possible, and we didn't get three seats together. So Lloyd sat alone across the aisle from me and his sister, who was again by the window. I still cried through takeoff, knowing what a baby I was. Even the flight attendant was laughing at me while I slept.

The airport in Minnesota was tiny. Since we had to go straight to the clinic, the airport had arranged a taxi. The drive only took twenty minutes and we arrived on time, an impressive feat considering our appointment was at 10:00 a.m. Man, were we ever tired! We even had to carry our luggage through the clinic.

We finally figured out where we were going and Lloyd checked in with the haematologist's office. The nurse took us back to the doctor's room and then told us he was with another patient and would be there soon. We sat there and waited. And waited. The wait seemed like an eternity. Lloyd's sister and I took turns sleeping on each other's shoulders. Neither of us seemed to really care about how tired poor Lloyd was.

Finally the doctor came in and took down Lloyd's history, dates of occurrences, etc. before examining him.

"I've never seen a relapse of ITP this bad before," he said. "But rest assured, I can help."

He went over Lloyd's options and explained that he would like to admit him to the hospital immediately and start treatments.

Then the big question came out of Lloyd's mouth: "How much will all this cost?"

Lloyd's biggest concern was money. Mine was getting him better. I didn't care how much things would cost; we would find a way.

We spoke with the doctor about our financial status, since Lloyd was already on short-term disability and money was pretty tight. That said, I told him we had a great support system back home and money wouldn't be an issue.

The doctor explained to us that the treatments would be as follows: R-CVP (Rituxan), cyclophosphamide (the chemo pill he had already been taking), vincristine (another chemo drug), and prednisone (which he was already taking). All this would be done through IV.

He explained that this would provide the most effective treatment to start. The Rituxan would be a four-week treatment, starting today and continuing for the next three Fridays.

Then the bomb hit. These four Rituxan treatments would cost $20,000 alone. That was in addition to the other treatments, plus the hospital stay, bloodwork, plus plus plus. We were looking at around $40,000 by the time it was all said and done.

The doctor assured us that he would do his best to keep costs down as much as possible.

Next we needed to get admitted and introduced to the team, including the doctor who would be taking good care of him through the weekend. So off we went!

We made it as far as the waiting room before Lloyd sat down in a chair.

"What's wrong?" I asked.

"Julie, we can't afford this. We can't do this."

"Don't worry about it. The money shouldn't be an issue."

I called my dad and got both my parents on the phone. I then explained everything the doctor had told us, adding how worried Lloyd was about the money. As usual, they told me not to worry about it. My dad set my mind at ease by assuring me that anything we needed would be taken care of. My dad always made me feel better.

I don't know about all the other women out there, but when I'm sad or broken-hearted and need a hug or shoulder to cry on, I go to my mom and always have. But when I'm experiencing tough times, confusion, or weakness, and when I need protection, I go to my dad.

When I got off the phone, I told Lloyd not to worry; he just needed to concentrate on getting better.

Lloyd was admitted right away and got a room to himself. He was given such good treatment from all the nurses.

But I remember sitting in his room on the couch and feeling really overwhelmed. Lloyd's sister and I finally decided to get a room in the hotel across the street to stay for the night. The hospital was connected to it by underground tunnels. And conveniently, there was a coffee shop right on the corner.

I told Lloyd that we were going to check in and take a shower and get something to eat, even though I didn't want to leave his side for a minute. All of a sudden, I saw a look of terror in his eyes. He told me to hurry up, that he needed me to be there with him.

Oh my gosh, that scared me even more. He didn't want to be alone even for five minutes.

We decided to go anyway, but we were quick about it.

When we got back to the hospital, nothing had happened, which was good. I didn't want to miss anything, and I didn't want him to go through it alone.

We were faced with another scary situation, though. The doctors had explained to us the side effects of taking Rituxan. Because it was still experimental, there was a one percent chance of dying while it was being administered. Now, I know one percent sounds like no big deal. But when you're faced with that possibility, it sounded like such a big deal. Obviously Lloyd was willing to take that chance, and so was I.

The doctors and nurses came in and explained how the treatments would work. They were going to administer one medication at a time and wait for each to finish until administering the next. Since this was his first time, they had to check his vitals with each dose to make sure he was doing okay.

They started with the cyclophosphamide, which didn't take very long. So far so good. Then they administered vincristine, and again he seemed fine. Next came the prednisone. Everything was going smoothly.

They hadn't started treatment until about 10:00 p.m. and I was beat. But I wanted to make sure he had the Rituxan before I left. This was the one I felt concerned about. I wanted to be right there by his side.

Finally the time came and they started to administer the Rituxan. I remember crawling into bed beside him and just lying there. Throughout these treatments, I never heard him complain once. He didn't complain about being tired. He didn't complain about a single thing.

The Rituxan was going to take a couple of hours, however, and by this time I was falling asleep. Lloyd's sister was already asleep on the couch, so she and I decided to go back over to the hotel. We were no good to him if we were that tired. Lloyd was falling asleep anyway, so we left. He was in good hands and the nurses had our phone number if anything should change.

I don't think I slept more than two hours that night. All I could do was cry. I regretted so much not staying over at the hospital. I hadn't even known that was an option. How could I have left? I felt like the worst wife in the world.

I kept going over these thoughts, all the while expecting the phone to ring at any minute telling me to get right over to the hospital. I swore after this night that I would never leave him again. I didn't care if I had to sleep on the floor from here on out.

First thing the next morning, we hurried over to the hospital. As usual, Lloyd was in good spirits. His night hadn't been too bad, even though he hadn't gotten much sleep with the nurses coming in to check his vitals and take blood all the time. He was very tired.

When his bloodwork came back, his platelets were still very low. Nothing had changed. But what could we expect? The treatments hadn't even worked through his system yet.

Lloyd was in the hospital all weekend and would get discharged Monday morning. On Saturday and Sunday, his sister and I were able to stay with him in his room. The couch pulled out into a bed and the staff wheeled a cot in for me. He had his own private bathroom, room service, and a TV and VCR. We were able to go down to the library and rent movies. We really couldn't have asked for better service.

Even the service at the hotel was amazing. We had originally checked in for the weekend, but when I explained our situation they only charged us for the first night.

The cost of the hospital room for one night was $1,070 and Lloyd was there three full days. Therefore, the cost of the room alone came to $3,210. That was a very expensive hotel stay! Of course, Lloyd was upset over the cost, but I explained to him that I wasn't upset and he shouldn't be either. We would figure it out. Somehow I knew we would be okay.

Throughout the weekend, we just lay around watching movies and eating very well. Everyone took good care of us. The room service was only meant for patients, but the three of us ordered enough food to feed an army. The kitchen knew what we were doing but let us get away with it. That's what I mean when I say they took such good care of us. I felt comfortable and safe there.

Very early Sunday morning, at 3:00 a.m., I clearly remember the "blood lady," as Lloyd called her, coming into the room. Because of how low his platelets were, and because of all the prednisone he had been on in the past, Lloyd's veins were few and far between. The woman had a heck of a time trying to get his blood; it was like trying to get blood from a stone. She actually had to call in the head nurse to get his blood, since nobody could do it.

I lay beside him on the cot and didn't let him know I was awake. I couldn't believe the pain he was going through just for the staff to try to draw blood. But again, he didn't complain. He cried a little bit but didn't complain once. It got so bad that one nurse had to put a blood pressure cuff on his arm and pump up his arm to bring out the veins. I was so grossed out when they did that.

They finally got the blood they needed, but wouldn't you know it… they had to come back again in an hour because either that blood reading didn't take or there hadn't been enough blood in the sample. Poor Lloyd had to go through it all over again.

The results came back within the hour. I remember Lloyd getting so frustrated when there was no improvement. The doctor came in and explained to us that the treatment would take time to work. I understood this, but for some reason Lloyd figured he should be feeling better and see results right away. The doctor told us that sometimes it could take up to four months for the Rituxan to start working. I was trying to be the voice of reason, but there was no reasoning with Lloyd; he wanted results and wanted them now.

I think the worst part of this experience for him was that the kids always wanted to talk to both of us when I called home. I'd start to cry because I missed them so much and Lloyd would cry because he didn't know if he would ever see them again. I truly believe that was the hardest part for him.

I knew the kids were fine and didn't worry about them once. My parents were staying with them at our house and we had a great support system, including Lloyd's parents, my sister and brother-in-law, and my cousin and his wife. So many people were there for Lloyd and me, and for our parents too. I thought about the kids and missed them terribly, but I was glad they weren't with us. I was there for Lloyd and wanted to concentrate only on him.

Of course, we had a few laughs here and there. One thing about Lloyd's sister was that she could always make me laugh. She and I have been known to be goofy and it was so refreshing when she acted that way. I don't know what I would have done if she hadn't been there with me.

Sunday happened to be Valentine's Day, and when the evening came Lloyd got a pass to go out for supper. He was so ready to take it. Everything was within walking distance, so the three of us walked to a restaurant. But by the time we got there, Lloyd was in tears and feeling very weak. He got dizzy and his nose started to bleed. In fact, he broke down right in the middle of the street. I just put my arms around him and hugged him, but he wasn't interested in hugging me, he was so darn angry.

What a breakthrough, part of me was thinking. *He's actually getting mad and reacting to what's happening to him!*

Until this point, he hadn't gotten angry—and I think it's okay to get angry. I think it's okay to get upset. After all, he was fighting for his life. He had every right to be angry.

The treatments didn't appear to be working, since he was still bleeding from every orifice. I understood that the treatments might take a while, but he just wasn't getting it. I let him get mad and blow off some steam. He needed to do that.

After about ten minutes, we went into the restaurant to eat supper. From what I can remember, it was quite expensive. We got something like an iced tea and soup and it cost something stupid, which made Lloyd even madder. We were spending unnecessary money.

He was more than ready after supper to go back to his room and lie down. We were all in bed early that night, especially since he was anxious to get out of the hospital the next morning.

Valentine's Day soon came and went and Lloyd said to me, "My Valentine's Day present is me getting better." Wow, what a gift! I used to complain about the cheesy gifts he bought me for Valentine's Day, and he sometimes wouldn't even remember them, but this year all I wanted was for him to survive.

After he got discharged from the hospital on Monday, we had an appointment with the original doctor we had seen upon our arrival on Friday. We had all been under the impression that we would be able to go home once Lloyd got discharged.

Nope, not even close.

His platelets had gone up a little, but not by enough for Lloyd to get excited about it. Of course, I thought any little improvement was great.

The Rituxan needed to be administered for the next three Fridays. I started to panic, thinking about us having to be there for the next three weeks. The doctor then explained that we could stay for the whole week, with Lloyd being monitored and continuing getting bloodwork so he could get his second Rituxan treatment as an outpatient.

In this process, we had a social worker trying her hardest to get as much money taken off the bill as possible. She was in contact with us pretty much every day to let us know what she was working on. I'm telling you, we got more help in the U.S. than we ever got in Canada. The social worker even put in a request to the drug company responsible for giving us

Rituxan, to cover the cost of the drug. Lloyd had to meet certain requirements, such as income and expenses. When she came back and told us that the drugs would be covered, Lloyd and I both cried in relief. That was $20,000 we didn't have to worry about. It's amazing how great and understanding everyone was.

When we left the hospital, we needed to find a place to stay for the rest of the week. We found the perfect spot, and it was connected to the underground tunnel leading right to the Mayo Clinic itself. The price was good and it was close to everything.

The next few days were spent just catching up on sleep and trying to get our finances in order. The doctor mentioned that we had to come back each Friday for treatment—that was, unless we could find somebody in Canada to administer it.

We couldn't pull that off, but certainly not from lack of trying. There were too many technicalities. We got in contact with Lloyd's doctor and nurse back in Oshawa. They even tried getting someone in a clinic in Buffalo to administer the drug. It couldn't be done in Canada, since Rituxan wasn't approved in Canada for ITP.

The really stupid part is it was available for people with lymphoma. Lloyd had once been at the hospital in Oshawa to get his treatments and saw his doctor administer Rituxan to a patient right beside him. It didn't seem fair, and we certainly didn't understand the rules and policies around this drug. Health Canada saw Rituxan as experimental. For them to cover our treatments in the U.S., we would have needed to request permission before going. But there hadn't been time for that.

Anyway, nobody was willing to administer the drug in Buffalo either. We found a cancer clinic, but the doctor needed to meet with Lloyd and assess him first—and that would have clearly taken too long, since we needed to make sure Lloyd got the Rituxan each Friday.

We discussed this issue with my parents and decided to come back down to the Mayo Clinic for the next three weeks. At least we had gotten one issue resolved, with the Rituxan being paid for. But then another issue would always arise. Would we ever catch a break?

According to the bloodwork Lloyd got done on Wednesday, his platelets were up. It was now clear that the treatments were starting to work. This boosted his mood a bit and we even rented a car for two days just to get out. It was nice to see something other than the Mayo Clinic, the hospital, and the surrounding buildings. We got to visit a really nice restaurant one night, and we even managed to go shopping at an outlet mall close to the hotel.

Six

We made arrangements to fly back home Friday morning. The doctors knew we were anxious to get home and told us that Lloyd could have his second treatment on Thursday instead. They didn't think it would hurt to change the day this once. Even so, we figured it would be smart to wait until Friday to actually fly back, even though his treatment was scheduled for early Thursday morning. We wanted to make sure everything went okay. He would probably have been too tired immediately afterward anyway.

I got up with him Thursday morning and headed over to the outpatient area. The treatment usually lasted two to three hours. Lloyd got hooked up right away and didn't get bloodwork done. He didn't want to spend the money, and I guess he figured he could wait until we got home for that; he was always told that he could come in anytime, even without an appointment.

I, on the other hand, was very curious to know what his platelet levels would be. I would have been willing to spend the money, but I had to wait.

The treatment was a success and we headed off to make our final travel arrangements. We made sure to get a wakeup call from the front desk. Lloyd's dad even phoned to ensure we didn't miss our flight.

The shuttle to the airport took at least forty-five minutes. I'll never forget it. We were sitting in the very back of a van, sandwiched into each other with a stranger on the left of me and Lloyd's sister on the right. The stranger kept falling asleep, her head lowering on my shoulder. Lloyd's sister just laughed. And of course every bump nearly shook us right out of our seats.

We got to the airport and went through the usual screenings. Soon we were waiting at the gate, with me getting nervous and nauseous again. This time I took Gravol.

At least the flight was direct this time. But it was such a little plane and very hot that the Gravol did nothing for me. I got sick and once again bore the brunt of all Lloyd and his sister's jokes.

When the plane landed, I had never been so glad to see Toronto in all my life. Lloyd's aunt and uncle came to pick us up from the airport, and I was so excited to be home that I could hardly contain myself. Lloyd wanted to stop at the hospital and get his bloodwork done, as well as to let all the nurses and the doctor know how everything had gone. I went in with him and found that the nurses were so happy to see that he'd survived. He got his bloodwork done and they told us to go home and see our kids; they would phone with the results when they got them back.

I don't think the car was completely stopped in our driveway when Lloyd and I jumped out and ran inside to see the kids. They both rushed into our arms. It felt like heaven to see them, to hug them, to kiss them. I hadn't thought it was possible to love my children more than I already did, but we just held them, sobbing. It was so good to be home!

About a half-hour, Lloyd's doctor's nurse called to tell us that his platelets were up to 97,000. Wow! That was the highest they had been in a long time. Clearly the doctors at the Mayo Clinic were geniuses, and clearly the treatments had worked.

I was so excited that I started to scream on the phone. Even the nurse had so much excitement in her voice. This truly felt like a happy ending. We were so high on adrenaline that we could barely contain ourselves.

That's when Lloyd's mom and dad arrived. They started crying when they heard the good news.

Once everybody had left, we truly started to breathe out in relief. I remember just sitting around for the longest time with the kids, taking them in, hugging them, and shedding tears of joy. It really felt like we had just woken up from a bad dream. It all felt so surreal.

We still had to figure out how he was going to get the next two treatments, though. The cancer clinic in Buffalo hadn't panned out. So my father, as awesome of a man as he is, decided to drive Lloyd all the way to Minnesota for the next treatment. At first we thought he was crazy, but he was trying to save us money.

Since Lloyd had to be there for Friday, they left Thursday morning bright and early. It was going to be a fifteen-hour drive. They drove through the night and took turns behind the wheel. But if you talk to my dad, he would tell you that he drove the whole time and Lloyd slept.

The weather was once again on our side. God and His angels took care of the situation and got them there safely. We couldn't have been more blessed with mother nature, especially since it was February.

On Friday morning, Lloyd had his treatment and my dad went in with him. This really surprised me because my dad was somewhat afraid of hospitals and doctors; he had pretty much watched all of his family and his friends die of some sort of cancer. But he went in with Lloyd. I thought this showed great courage and support. I know for a fact that it meant the world to Lloyd, since they had a love/hate relationship. They were the best of friends… but when one of them disagreed with the other, we all heard about it. They both always thought they were right. My mom and I often joked about Lloyd and my dad being married to each other, the way they bickered back and forth. Then five minutes later, they would make plans to work on something together.

They ended up getting a hotel room for the night, since they were so exhausted. I can't blame them. I think they found something to eat and then got into bed to sleep by 4:00 p.m. They then woke up bright and early and headed home without any bad weather—or any other problem, for that matter. Lloyd pretty much rested the whole next week.

When he went into the hospital for bloodwork, I recall that his platelets had actually dropped. He still had one more treatment, though, and we just focused on trying to figure out how to get back down to Mayo. Neither one of us wanted my dad to drive again. He would have done it, but we wouldn't let him.

We realized we would have no choice but to fork out the money to fly. But then some friends of my parents gave us some free Air Miles. How generous! Just when things were getting frustrating again, someone came along and saved the day. Angels in disguise, that's who these people were. Truly angels. They know who they are and I have nothing but the highest respect for them. They've known me since I was five years old and I refer to them as my second parents. I love them for what they did to help us out. They're always there for me and my family.

So the following Thursday, we flew back down to Mayo. Lloyd's appointment once again was scheduled for Friday morning. We actually planned on coming back on Saturday instead of Friday, in case things didn't quite go well, or in case Lloyd was too tired. It felt like a bit of a holiday for me, even though it wasn't, even though the circumstances were awful. It was nice to get away, just the two of us.

When we landed at the airport, this time we got a rental car. That way we didn't have to depend on anyone else to get around. We stopped off at a restaurant about halfway there to eat some supper. We then decided to stay in the same hotel where Lloyd and my dad had stayed. It was about a ten-minute drive to the hospital.

Upon our arrival, I went in to book a room for the night. As a bonus, the hotel had a pool and a hot tub. That sounded so good to me! I was glad I had packed our bathing suits.

Once we got settled in, I was dying to go swimming and just sit and relax. I am stunned and amazed to this day at how well God took care of Lloyd during this time, because as it turned out his platelets were deathly low.

When the Mayo nurses took blood from him on Friday morning, Lloyd said to me, "Could you imagine if I had fallen and bumped my head while swimming last night? I would have been bleeding from the brain right now."

That's all I could think about. My goodness. What had we been thinking, going swimming? He was right. What if something had happened? Well, it hadn't. After that, we were a little more cautious. We thought about every possible consequence.

Lloyd slept through his whole treatment, which took about three hours. They had TVs hooked up to each bed, as well as free movies. I was so uncomfortable in the chair I sat in, but I tried not to complain—because no matter how uncomfortable I was, how did Lloyd feel? And he never complained.

His treatment once again ended with success. There was no nausea, no vomiting, no pain, and basically no side effects. We ended up checking out of the hotel that morning and got a room at a nicer hotel for pretty much the same price. When we checked in, I remember lying on the bed and falling instantly asleep. That's how brutally tired I was. Lloyd had some unusual energy and felt like going shopping, but all I wanted to do was sleep.

After about two hours of him sitting there watching TV and watching me sleep, he woke me up and we went out for supper and shopped. When we got back, neither of us wanted to go swimming. We knew better this time! So we just crawled into bed and watched TV for the night. I remember having to be up early to drive back to the airport to catch our flight. All I could think about was how glad I would be when this was all over.

Lloyd had bloodwork appointments on March 2 and March 11, and each time we were disappointed and frustrated to find that his platelets were still quite low, especially after they'd been so high after the second treatment. It seemed they had dropped again for no reason. He started to get down and I had to remind him about what the doctor at the Mayo Clinic had said: "It will take time. Don't get discouraged." I could see and understand this, but Lloyd was impatient. I can't really blame him. He had been through so much and wanted to get back to some kind of normal.

At his March 14 checkup, his platelets rose to 54, which the doctors considered to be in the "safe" range. For the next couple of weeks, they kept rising and rising. He even got excited about going back to work. The doctor told him to slow down and not be in such a hurry, since he and his body had been through so much, but Lloyd was secretly planning to work anyway. He was ready to go back to his old routine.

Just when we thought things were really looking up, something went terribly wrong.

Lloyd started feeling very tired and lethargic and didn't look all that great. At an appointment for bloodwork, he mentioned to the doctor how he was feeling and the bloodwork showed his haemoglobin to be slightly low. This was on March 18, at a time when his platelets were up to 160, finally in the normal range.

Bear in mind that the normal range for a man's haemoglobin count is 130–165. It's measured the same as platelets, in the thousands.

Well, on March 2 his haemoglobin count had been 149,000. On March 11, when his platelets were very low, his haemoglobin came in at 123,000. But no one picked up on it at the time because they were so focused on his platelet count.

After looking back on his bloodwork, there was a definite pattern with his haemoglobin: it had been slowly dropping.

On March 29, Lloyd was tested positive for autoimmune haemolytic anaemia, another autoimmune disease, just like ITP. He tested positive +2, which essentially meant he had bad antibodies floating around in his system. The higher the positive, the more antibodies a person has.

With these haemoglobin problems, Lloyd was experiencing new symptoms, including loss of breath. His skin started turning yellow because his liver was being affected. The whites in his eyes were turning yellow as well. He was so tired that he was sleeping around the clock. He couldn't get enough sleep.

The doctor knew that this was out of his hands and Lloyd needed a specialist. He got a hold of a specialist at Sunnybrook Hospital in Toronto and they made an appointment for him to come down in April.

Once again we played the waiting game. In the meantime, I phoned the doctor at the Mayo Clinic and discussed Lloyd's condition with him. The doctor told me that Lloyd had something called Evan's Syndrome. Unfortunately, when someone has one autoimmune disease, they are more susceptible to developing others. He also told me he would be able to help again if we wanted to come back down.

The doctor in Oshawa hooked up Lloyd to oxygen to help with his breathing. Someone from the Durham Region Home

Oxygen Centre came over with a huge oxygen tank with tubes and a big book explaining everything.

This couldn't possibly be happening. The kids were scared out of their minds. They didn't know what was going on. I was trying to be strong for Lloyd, but mostly for my kids.

This was all new to me. I had learned everything there was to know about ITP, but now I had to learn everything about autoimmune haemolytic anaemia. That was a mouthful! I needed to understand how it was affecting Lloyd's red blood cells and oxygen levels. When your haemoglobin is low, it means you don't have enough red blood cells to deliver and carry oxygen to the body, including the heart and lungs. It's very similar to ITP, regarding the red blood cells being eaten up like Pacman.

When the guy came to hook up the oxygen tank and show Lloyd what to do, I could barely keep myself from crying. This wasn't right. He had already been through hell and back—and survived. Now it was happening all over again.

After the guy left, Lloyd went to bed. He was so tired that he could barely talk. I told him that I would go over to my parents' house to give him some peace and quiet. When I got the kids in the car, though, and pulled out of the driveway, the tears started flowing. I kept praying and praying, basically begging God to keep Lloyd safe. He seemed to have escaped death the first time, but what was going to happen to him now?

I pulled into my parents' driveway and found them waiting for us outside. They had known I was coming over.

I got out of the car and walked right over to them. They had their arms open to me and the three of us just stood there, hugging and crying. They knew what I was feeling. We didn't have to speak. Once again I felt scared, overwhelmed, and confused.

Seven

The next few weeks proved to be very challenging. We had Delaney's birthday party; she was turning four. I was going to cancel it, but Lloyd wanted to have everyone in. He didn't want to stop life just because he was sick. He felt Delaney needed her party amongst all the fear and anxiety around us.

The day finally arrived when we headed up to Sunnybrook Hospital. Everyone there was amazing. Lloyd didn't have to wait long for anything. The staff was on the ball and did their homework. Lloyd got bloodwork done and his haemoglobin was down to 60. Very deathly low. The doctors then told Lloyd that this autoimmune disease could be worse than having ITP.

Worse? Were they kidding me? What we had just been through hadn't even been the worst of it? Well, it turns out that when your haemoglobin drops down to 40, you have to watch very carefully for signs of cardiac arrest. Great! Now Lloyd could have a heart attack.

One thing we hadn't known during our time at the Mayo Clinic was that people with chronic ITP and platelets can suffer strokes, seizures, blood pressure problems, and heart problems. Amazingly, Lloyd hadn't experienced any of this. But from our research, we learned that lots of people with ITP suffered in these ways. So nobody can ever tell me that God isn't real. I believe that God kept Lloyd from experiencing these conditions. Don't ask me why. I don't have the answers. All I know is that God was with us every step of the way and was very faithful in answering our prayers.

The doctors at Sunnybrook were optimistic that their treatments would work. They didn't see any reason for us to go back to the Mayo Clinic, and this was music to our ears. They went through the various options, but the first treatment option was another high dose of prednisone. That seemed to be a very popular treatment. They told Lloyd to try this for a while. Then, if it didn't work, he could have another round of Rituxan, cyclophosphamide, vincristine, and prednisone.

It only took two to three weeks of prednisone treatments for his haemoglobin to climb back into the normal range. By the end of May 2005, everything was stable. Lloyd went back to work, feeling so happy to be back. I remember Lloyd's first day. I got up with him, made him breakfast, and walked him out to the car. It was like my kid's first day of school. I cried as he drove down the road. It was kind of bittersweet.

The doctor kept a very close eye on him with regularly scheduled bloodwork. And things changed at work. Lloyd no longer had any managerial duties or responsibilities. It wasn't a demotion, just a reduction in stress. Now he was actually able to leave work every day at 5:00 p.m., as opposed to before when he rarely made it home for supper. Sometimes he even called me from work at 3:00 p.m. and complained about being bored. In the past, I had never been able to get him to call me from work. He was far too busy. They were really taking it easy on him, which was fine with me! He had been through hell and back, having to take so many drugs.

I can't express how awesome and generous people were throughout his ordeal. God had moved so much in our lives, bringing friends and families together. People from church we didn't even really know would drop off supper for us. There actually is some good in this screwed-up world!

With Lloyd back at work, we tried getting into the swing of things again, but we were faced with the giant Mayo Clinic bill. We had to make a $500 credit card payment every month.

When we'd first arrived at the Mayo Clinic, they had told us to pay for everything upfront. This had been overwhelming, even impossible. Paying $20,000 before Lloyd was even seen? We had been forced to explain that we couldn't do it. The people there had been very understanding. We started with a deposit to see the doctor and followed this with monthly payments. These payments started in March, when Lloyd was still on short-term disability.

Upon leaving Mayo, we were given six months to pay off the total. Six months seems like forever, but it went by so fast, especially when Lloyd returned to work.

Throughout this time, we never struggled to buy what we needed, including groceries. Our story is a testimony to God's goodness and provision. He was in control of everything. I never got mad at Him once while Lloyd was sick. Yes, I questioned Him and didn't understand why any of this was happening, but I trusted Him. I never quit trusting Him.

To this day, I still don't understand why this all happened, but God must have had a master plan.

Lloyd was the strongest person I knew. I had thought I knew him before, but through this experience I realized that I had more to learn about his strength, his fight, and his courage. It made me want to be a better person. When I looked at Lloyd, I saw my hero.

Once the six months were up, we received a final notice from the Mayo Clinic to pay the remaining bill in full. We couldn't manage this, so I called the office to find out whether we could extend the payments.

Basically, we had two options. The first was to pay the full $17,000 and be done with it. If we extended the payments, they would have to increase to the range of $800 to $900 per month. But who has that kind of money to shell out monthly?

We decided to take the first option and take out a loan from the bank. Thank God that Lloyd was back to work by now, which helped with the approval process. With this money, we were able to gladly hand over the money and reduce our Mayo balance to zero. I say that we handed it over gladly because if it hadn't been for the Mayo Clinic and what they did for Lloyd, he wouldn't have been alive. Yes, it was an atrocious amount of money, but it had been worth it. I would have done the same thing all over again.

Our government hadn't been too kind in helping out. We submitted all our paperwork to the Minister of Health, hoping to get our costs reimbursed. All we were asking for was the $17,000. That didn't include the cost of flights, hotels, or food. I think we were pretty reasonable.

We worked closely with our Member of the Provincial Parliament at the time, John O'Toole, who did everything possible to get all or some of our money back. He spoke in the Legislative Assembly and wrote numerous letters to the Minister of Health about our case.

The Ministry wouldn't budge. They refused to reimburse us for two main reasons: apparently Lloyd had needed to be preapproved before leaving Canada for treatment and Rituxan was still considered experimental. We went to the appeals board and argued that we hadn't had time to wait to be preapproved. They still denied us.

This situation made it hard for us to say we were proud to be Canadian. We were both born here, made a good living, paid taxes, and worked hard. And when one of us contracted a life-threatening illness, our so-called government wouldn't help. So am I proud and happy to be a Canadian citizen? I don't say that. We might as well have lived in the United States. Of course we are lucky to live in Canada, the home of the free. It's a beautiful country. But I do feel jaded and resentful. Canada failed us. Canada failed to protect and help its own.

George Canyon has a song called "Who Would You Be?" This song is symbolic to our family. It describes a man who would rather be a perfect husband and father, the world's greatest dad, than anything else in life. That is what Lloyd strived for. He loved his family more than anything.

When I heard this song for the first time, I thought to myself, who would I choose to be? I looked at my husband and told myself, *I choose to be him. He is truly my hero. He is the strongest, most courageous person in the world. He came through the worst nightmare in his life with even more strength than before. He never once complained or felt sorry for himself.*

When I get a cold or the flu, I feel like I'm going to die. After being through what we went through, though, you take an oath to never complain again, to never take anything for granted, not even once. I came out of this experience loving life more, loving people more. I enjoyed my kids more. I didn't want to fight or argue. The things that really mattered, mattered more. The little things that really shouldn't matter didn't matter anymore.

If there is a lesson to be learned here, it's simply this: love life more and don't take a single day for granted. I do believe that God has a master plan. Our patience and faith were tested and I still believe that God is working in our lives and making all things new.

Lloyd was a daily reminder to me of how short life is. I was reminded of this when I looked at the huge scar on his stomach, from when he'd had his spleen removed back in 2001. For the longest time, too, he had a bruise on his back. He couldn't see it, but I looked at it every day; it wouldn't go away, just like the nightmare we had gone through.

But at this point in our story, it *had* gone away. We knew Lloyd would relapse, and when he did he would be even stronger and more knowledgeable about ITP and the treatments available. We would also have a more positive attitude towards the whole situation.

Eight

Soon we were in a brand-new year. Lloyd had been in remission since May 2005 and been going for regular checkups. He had also done a lot of research regarding ITP and how to keep healthy. Of course, nobody knew exactly what to do to stay healthy and nobody could know for sure what would cause a relapse. All we could do was talk to other ITP patients and keep researching. Lloyd visited the ITP chatline and found people who had tried tanning, eating more green vegetables, and taking more vitamins and supplements. Lloyd tried all of these. He got a lot of support from these chats. They gave him people apart from me to discuss the disease and everything we had gone through.

We noticed that he seemed to relapse only in the wintertime, which led to a theory that he didn't get enough vitamin D from sunlight. So that's why he started tanning. We didn't know for sure if this would work, but we knew it couldn't hurt to try. And he had been stable for a while.

So many people had been supportive throughout the last year. I didn't know where to start. The people at our church had learned of our financial problems; when you're on short-term disability, you don't make much money. This is why I need to recognize a few people from our church for helping us in our time of need. They decided to host a benefit concert to raise money for our living expenses. Because of them, I can say that we didn't struggle once with money, nor did we ever wonder where our next meal was coming from. God sent us people who knew what our needs were. They helped us beyond what we needed.

I will never forget the night of the benefit concert. I was so overwhelmed with emotion. At least two hundred people came, and I would say Lloyd and I only knew fifty of them. Friends of ours performed most of the music. There were also a few other singers, and even an Elvis impersonator. The room was filled with God's presence! His hope was with us all.

Lloyd and I had to get up for a few minutes and speak. It wasn't that hard for me, because I'm a public speaker, but Lloyd was nervous. Once I'd said what I had to say, Lloyd took the microphone from me. This surprised me, because I hadn't thought he would say much of anything at all. He started talking about his experience and then thanked me for everything. I could hardly keep from crying.

The whole night was like that for me. The tears were right there, ready to be let go.

No words can really describe what happened at the end of the night. When the church took up a collection, I was under the impression that we would find out at a later date how much money had been raised. But at the end of the evening, the man in charge asked everybody to stand up. He needed to make an announcement.

I had no idea what he was going to say. I was stunned when he opened an envelope and started to choke up. Then he announced that they had raised $3,300 for us.

I thought I was going to pass out. Lloyd and I started crying, and the whole congregation clapped. Before the benefit, a reporter from the local newspaper had come out to interview us. Our story and picture appeared in the paper.

Well, it turned out that people from all over the region had donated money, people we didn't even know. Like I said, no words can express our gratitude for everyone who was a part of our ordeal.

After the church fundraiser, my sister organized a dance in June 2005 at which they raised $2,300. Again, it was an overwhelming night for us. Lloyd didn't like to be the centre of attention, but that night I decided to sing for him. I called him onstage and sang like it was just the two of us in the room. We just kept looking into each other's eyes. In those moments, he was the only one who mattered to me. I sang Keith Urban's "Making Memories of Us."

This was a very humbling experience, and an amazing thing my sister did for us. It was a great night to get together with friends and family.

Our families have been a huge support. I couldn't have done this without the support of my family, and Lloyd felt the same way. He was doing well and feeling good. Our story had come to a happy ending, despite the reality that many other people's stories didn't end up happy. I just hoped and prayed we would never have to journey down the same road again. For myself, I came out on the other side a better person, but we were both trying hard to figure out the meaning behind it. We desperately needed to make sense of this.

"Maybe this happened to me so I can help other people the way people have helped me," Lloyd told me one day.

Wow! I thought to myself. *That is so amazing of him. What a great outlook he has about the whole thing. He truly is my hero, my husband whom I am so proud of and love with all my heart.*

Our experiences had made us stronger in many ways. Stronger as a married couple, stronger as individuals, stronger as parents, and stronger in our walk with God.

As the calendar turned to 2006, I continued to pray for Lloyd's health and for a better year ahead. I wanted to support all the others who were fighting the same terrible blood disease.

My heart went out to everyone going through what Lloyd had gone through.

Our lives had changed so much. Since his relapse, we had decided to live life to the fullest, expressing gratitude for every single day God had granted us.

Well, that ended tragically.

People say that they never forget certain dates in their lives that are of particular importance—like 9/11 or the day Kennedy was shot.

But one day stands out for me. July 18, 2006.

The day my husband died.

Nine

The new years was going smoothly. Lloyd had settled into a new job close to home, and once the nice weather hit he started rollerblading to work. I asked him every day if he wanted me to pick him up, but he never accepted my offer. He wanted to persevere. Part of me thought he was crazy, and the other part of me was so proud. I kept thinking that I could never do that. Each way was about fourteen miles!

It started to get hot right at the beginning of summer. I figured it was going to be a really hot summer, like the last, and I couldn't help but be a little worried about him rollerblading in the heat.

With this new job, Lloyd got every other Friday off. On one of these Fridays, everything changed. I remember every single thing that happened from that day on, just like it happened yesterday. It's incredibly hard to relive it, but I'm hoping that someone reading this will be touched and find comfort in my words, just as I find strength and healing through writing them.

Friday, July 14 was incredibly hot. I remember waking up that morning so grateful to have Lloyd home. We had been planning to go to the cottage the previous night and spend the weekend there, but at the last minute we'd decided to stay. Gas was so expensive and we thought we could put that money to better use.

We had bought season passes to Canada's Wonderland, a popular amusement park north of Toronto. We thought about maybe going there, but then decided against it because of the heat.

The final decision was to stay close to him. I took the kids over to my cousin's house to go swimming for the day. Meanwhile, Lloyd wanted to work in the garage. On Saturday night, we were going to attend another cousin's fortieth birthday party and she had asked Lloyd to be in charge of the music. Between garage work and getting the music together, he would be busy doing his own thing.

Obviously I didn't think anything would go wrong. It never occurred to me that this would be our last day together. If I had known, I wouldn't have left. But as I have been told in the months and years since, how can you anticipate something like this? I have dealt with a lot of guilt for leaving that day.

I was looking forward to going to my cousin's party the next night. It was going to be a good night out for us. We were going to take the kids so they could take part in the dancing. We had gone to another cousin's wedding the previous summer and didn't bring the kids. Lloyd had said the kids would come to the next function we attended, because they'd have so much fun. Lloyd and I always danced around at home. We always had the music on. He would pick up one kid and dance with her while I picked up the other. For the next song, we'd switch kids. That's how I had grown up, with my mom and dad always playing music in the house. Our house was anything but quiet growing up.

When we got home from swimming, Lloyd was sitting inside the air-conditioned house. I saw that he had cleaned up the garage, having swept a big pile of garbage right in the middle of the floor. He hadn't gotten to clean the pile yet, though, because he felt tired and had worked enough that day.

He told me that he'd even gone rollerblading. All the neighbours remembered seeing him skating around the block. I remember yelling at him for doing that because it was so hot out. He had even gone over to my parents' house because he had started a garden at the back of their property and wanted to do some work on it.

He didn't look any different to me. He wasn't acting any different, so there was no cause for alarm. Other than being tired, he seemed fine.

I went out and rented a movie for the night. Lloyd made supper while I put the kids to bed and he barbequed a nice steak. We sat outside just as the sun was going down. The evening was beautiful, peaceful, and calm. We both felt tired, having been outside all day, and I was quite sunburned. We had such a nice supper outside while the kids slept. We even lit some candles and opened a nice bottle of wine. I just chalked the exhaustion up to the heat.

Our neighbour had given us bunkbeds and we were going to set it up in Ella's bedroom. She was three now. Lloyd carried the bunkbeds upstairs and set them in the hall. After doing that, he had to sit down. He was so out of breath that he was huffing and puffing.

Again, I thought it was because of the temperature.

He told me that he would put the beds together in the morning.

We had a habit of changing things in our house and yard a lot. But while sitting out on our swing, we talked about how happy we were to have finally finished the backyard the way we wanted it.

We felt complete! Lloyd was happy and his health was good. Everything was well with the kids. We felt a sense of fullness, a feeling that nothing bad could happen. We felt invincible. I mean, we had already gone through the worst thing that could possibly happen. I guess I was pretty naïve to think that.

When we went to bed early that night, little did I know that it would be the last night my husband would sleep beside me in our bed.

On Saturday morning, Lloyd got up with the kids and let me sleep in. He usually did that, as he was the early riser, unlike me. When I got up, I went downstairs to find Lloyd sleeping in his chair and the kids playing in their playroom.

How mean am I? I thought to myself. I should have let him sleep in. Clearly he was still feeling the effects of the previous day's heat.

We started to go on with our day—that is, until Lloyd went to the bathroom. I soon heard him yelling from down the hall. The toilet was full of blood, which led us both to believe that his platelets were once again low.

Even though he'd had haemoglobin problems, we assumed this was a relapse of ITP. After all, you don't bleed with low haemoglobin!

As it had been with our old routine, I called his parents to drop off the kids on our way to the hospital. I was freaking out, but once again Lloyd was very calm.

When we got to the hospital, the staff took him in right away because of his condition. It seemed like we waited forever for the doctor—and when we saw her, the first thing I thought was that she reminded me of Doogie Howser. She seemed all of twelve years old!

Come on, I thought. *Can someone take us seriously please?*

She didn't know about Lloyd's condition. In fact, she was unfamiliar with both ITP and haemolytic anaemia.

Lloyd finally got bloodwork done. Lo and behold, his haemoglobin was down to 120, on the low end of normal. His platelets weren't a concern this time. Still, the low haemoglobin explained why he had been so tired and out of breath the day before.

I explained to the doctor that this wasn't normal for Lloyd, considering his history. His haemoglobin was clearly dropping. The doctor believed that he had an infection somewhere that was causing bleeding, which in turn was causing his haemoglobin to drop. She wanted to prescribe antibiotics and prednisone.

Lloyd said no. He wanted to wait until Monday so that he could see his haematologist. He had done some reading which suggested that taking antibiotics could lower a person's platelets. He didn't want to take that chance, since his platelet count was so good at the moment. I was kind of mad at him, because I thought he should be taking both antibiotics and prednisone and not wait until Monday, but he felt so strongly about it. I couldn't change his mind.

So off home we went, stopping to pick up the kids at his parents' house, as they lived close to the hospital. It still hadn't sunk in that this was bad, or that it was going to be bad, because while we were with his parents I got some clothes from his sister to wear to my cousin's birthday party. I still had it in my mind that we would go, at least for a bit.

"Come on, Julie," Lloyd kept saying. "Let's go. I have to go."

"Relax, I'll be there in a minute."

Nobody expected it to be so bad. He always got better after a relapse. It was routine by now; he would get sick, get treatment, then get better! Besides, we had already been through the worst of it.

He was so tired, though. All he wanted to do was go home to bed. I took him home and he went right to sleep. My poor husband could barely breathe, he was so out of breath. But once again, he didn't complain.

After he went to bed, I took the kids over to my parents' house and told them what the doctor had said and how completely frustrated I felt. Then I asked my parents to watch the kids for a few more minutes so I could go over to my cousin's house to pick up some stuff I had left there the day before when we'd gone swimming. But what I really wanted to do was vent and break down and cry, something I only felt comfortable doing with my cousin.

So that's what I did! I walked in and found them sitting around the table having coffee. After explaining about the hospital visit, I sat there and cried. All I could think about was that it was all happening again. But how could this be happening again? It didn't make any sense.

And yet not even once did I think we might lose him.

I picked up the kids and went back home to discover Lloyd still sleeping. He pretty much stayed in bed all day. He didn't eat anything and felt overall pretty crappy.

Later that night, he wanted me to take him back to the emergency room. My parents were at my cousin's party, so we dropped the kids off with Lloyd's parents and drove all the way back to the hospital in Oshawa.

We once again had to explain the whole situation. They took us in right away. The doctor who we saw felt concerned about Lloyd's prostate and wanted to set him up with an appointment Monday morning to see a urologist. They also ordered a CT scan to check for kidney stones. Whatever was going on in his body, it was making his haemoglobin drop.

But they didn't do any bloodwork, even though I asked. The doctor said there was no use since it had just been done that morning.

The CT scan showed nothing. Okay, so now what? We were starting from scratch again. The problem could be his prostate, but we would have to wait until Monday to find out. Or it could be an infection… but where and how bad was it?

Once again we were faced with the waiting game. None of the doctors could tell us what to do, so they sent us home.

I was so mad that the doctors hadn't asked for bloodwork. I had argued with the doctor, but it seemed like the more I pushed for it, the harder he pushed back. He just wouldn't listen.

I was so worried and scared. This was getting serious! I kept thinking about what we had gone through at the Mayo Clinic. But it wouldn't be as bad as that. Again, I just assumed we had already been through the worst of it.

When we got home, Lloyd went right to bed and I took his temperature. He had a low-grade fever.

Then, out of nowhere, he started to throw up. I started to think he might just have the flu. He felt really sick.

Okay. So he had the flu.

But that still didn't explain why he was bleeding every time he went pee. Was the flu making his haemoglobin drop?

We had no answers to any of these questions. I just didn't get it!

Sunday morning came and back to the hospital we went. The nurses took him right away for bloodwork. As expected, his haemoglobin had dropped to 19,000. They admitted him this time. He was so mad about that, since all he wanted to do was get some meds and go home. Even though he was getting more and more out of breath, he was still able to move around.

They hooked him up to an IV to get some fluids into him. At one point he was so mad about having to stay in the hospital that he took the IV pole and walked out into the hall demanding to see a doctor. When a doctor finally paid attention to him, he told Lloyd that absolutely under no circumstances would he go home when his haemoglobin was this low. He was still peeing blood and feeling very sick. The doctors were looking out for Lloyd's best interests. So back on the gurney he went and he settled down a bit.

I turned to Lloyd. "Maybe when this is all said and done and you're fine and out of the hospital, you should think about quitting your job and us putting the house up for sale and moving down to the cottage permanently."

He gave me an angry look. "Julie, I don't want to talk about this right now."

I tried pushing it, but he just got madder. I don't know whether he knew that he was going to die. I sure didn't. If he knew, he didn't let on to me. I was being very naïve in thinking that he was going to pull through because he always did. I thought we would follow through with my plan to move to my parents' cottage. That was his favourite place to be. It all made sense to me. He wouldn't have to worry about working, about being stressed or unhealthy. It sounded perfect.

I had spent the day with him, but it was getting late and his parents were coming up to see him. So he told me that I should go home and take care of the kids.

"No, I'm not leaving you," I said.

He insisted that I should go, that he would be fine—and yes, he was fine. Still peeing blood but otherwise in good humour, cracking jokes.

I kissed him goodbye and he assured me that he would call me later when he was finally in his room, since until now he had been in the emergency department. Then we did the trade-off. His parents came in and his sister dropped me and the girls off back at our house.

Once we were settled in, Lloyd's mom called me and informed me that he was stable. Lloyd also called to say that he was in a ward with four older men, one who snored. Lloyd complained about that but laughed at the same time. He told me that he loved me and the girls and wanted me to sleep tight. He would see me in the morning.

I pulled a mattress off Delaney's bed and put it in my room, so she and Ella could sleep close by that night. Delaney was only five and Ella three; they had no clue as to what was going on. I just told them that Daddy was in the hospital for the night and would be back home soon.

We put on a movie and eventually everyone fell asleep.

Ten

The phone rang at 6:00 a.m. Monday morning. It was Lloyd's nurse, explaining that he hadn't had a very good night and wasn't doing well. I should get to the hospital as soon as possible.

Were they kidding me? He had been fine when I left him. What had changed?

I called my parents right away to come pick me up. I then jumped in the shower. I don't know why I did that, but I did. As I walked into the bathroom, I was reminded of how serious Lloyd's condition was; there were blood stains all around the toilet from peeing. That image will always be embedded in my brain.

I got into the shower and stood there crying. At times I even screamed. For the first time in the five years since this nightmare had begun I was beginning to think I might really lose him.

Lloyd's sister stayed with the kids and made arrangements with my cousin and his wife to pick them up so she and Lloyd's parents could come to the hospital later in the day.

When my mom picked me up, I remember her driving like a maniac to get me to the hospital as quickly as possible. You would have to know my mom to understand this. She was a little scared to drive and was behind the wheel of my dad's big truck—jumping curbs, speeding, and blasting through stop signs. Looking back, it was kind of funny. Normally she was the most cautious driver ever.

Lloyd was in the first room off to the left as soon as I stepped through the doors of the emergency department. As soon as I walked in and saw him lying there, I thought I was going to be sick. My mom called our pastor so he could come to the hospital. Lloyd was completely jaundiced. Even his eyes were yellow. He was unresponsive.

He woke up when I went over to him and started talking. Meanwhile the doctor performed reflex tests on his feet. That was his most ticklish spot, so he nearly kicked the doctor in the head. At least we knew that he was aware of his surroundings!

My dad was scheduled for a colonoscopy that morning just down the hall, so my parents came in. They called my sister and asked her to come up from Peterborough as well. Lloyd's parents and sister were there now, too, as well as Lloyd's aunt and uncle.

He had a seizure right in front of everybody. I tell you, if you've never seen anyone have a seizure before, it's definitely something you could live without. I didn't know what was happening at first and started to scream and cry. Lloyd's aunt went ballistic and that freaked me out even more. The doctor explained to me that the seizure was due to his haemoglobin being so low. He wasn't getting enough oxygen to his brain.

They decided to take him in for a CT scan of the brain to determine whether the seizure had done any permanent damage. We all sat out in the waiting room to wait.

My pastor had now arrived, and he and I talked privately off to the side. He quoted from Philippians 4:7: *"…and the peace of God, which surpasses all understanding, will guard your hearts and minds through Christ Jesus."* I guess it comforted me at the time, but it was many years before I really knew and understood what that scripture meant.

After the scan, we waited for a room to open up in the CCU (critical care unit). He'd had another seizure while on the table, but nothing abnormal had shown up in his brain.

My dad went in for his procedure thinking that Lloyd was going to be okay, because he always was. He had pulled through every emergency he'd gone through. He was tough and would be just fine. No one really grasped the severity of his condition or what was happening.

He finally got a room in the CCU. Lloyd's family and I went up to wait in the waiting room until he was set up and ready for company. The nurses were great in the CCU, very caring and compassionate. They didn't really understand his condition either but did everything they could to help and keep him comfortable.

When we went in, Lloyd was hooked up to the machine that showed all his stats, like blood pressure, heartbeat, and oxygen flow. He was also connected to an oxygen machine. When your haemoglobin is as low as his was, it's hard for your organs to keep going. These are the red blood cells that deliver oxygen to the heart and lungs. That's why his breathing was laboured; he didn't have enough red blood cells to deliver oxygen to his lungs.

They hooked him up to a catheter, too, and he was still peeing blood profusely. The doctor ordered seven units of red blood cells to be transfused. He peed that out as quickly as he received it.

The family was in and out of his room all day. He would be conscious for a while, then sleep. He remembered that my dad had undergone his colonoscopy that morning. When I took my mom back to see Lloyd, he was sleeping and we just sat there quietly with him.

"How is Poppy doing?" Lloyd asked when he woke up and saw my mom. Poppy… that's what my kids called my dad. When Lloyd said this, it made my mom cry. Even with everything he was going through, he was still thinking of my dad.

As the day went on, we could see Lloyd getting worse. The doctor was in several times and told me that he had an infection somewhere. They were thinking that maybe it was related to his bladder. But they couldn't treat the infection until they got his haemoglobin under control.

The conclusion the doctors reached was that Lloyd indeed had a bladder infection. They thought this was a side effect of the Rituxan he had taken a year and a half earlier at the Mayo Clinic. And wouldn't you know it? I looked it up and, yes, severe bladder infections are a side effect of that drug. They can happen a year later or even longer.

Well, what a kick in the head that was. He took one thing to prolong his life, and that very same thing was threatening him now. A bladder infection would be no big deal for a normal, working body. It would be totally treatable. But Lloyd's body was anything but normal. It was even dangerous for him to get a cold.

So there we had it—some kind of answer, or at least an educated guess. But it was all the doctors could go on, the only thing that somewhat made sense.

Still, nothing could be done. Not with his haemoglobin so low.

Back in the emergency room, the doctor told me that they wanted to intubate him to get his bleeding under control, as well as his breathing. I was against this. They had done an oxygen test which showed that his oxygen levels really weren't that bad. There didn't seem to be any justification yet for intubation.

But the doctor kept talking to me about it. Intubation would mean putting him on a ventilator so his body could get some rest. Once he was intubated, hopefully his body would start healing and they could treat the bladder infection.

The same doctor also asked whether Lloyd had a DNR (do not resuscitate) order. Was he kidding me? Of course they should resuscitate him!

"Do everything you can possibly do to keep him alive," I said.

I was really offended when he asked me that. but as my mother-in-law pointed out, it was his job to know what he was dealing with. Okay. So that made sense. But I was still offended and didn't much like this doctor after that.

The day passed into night and everyone went home except me and Lloyd's mom. He had been pretty much stable all day, even though his breathing was really bad and he was still peeing blood.

The nurses wheeled in a geriatric chair so I could sleep in Lloyd's room with him.

Things started to worsen as the night wore on, so Lloyd's mom called his dad and sister and told them to come back. I was instructed to go out of the room, too, because they needed to put a bigger, heavier breathing mask on him. His breathing was really laboured now.

As I sat out at one of the nurse's desks, I happened to turn and look at a computer screen. I'll never forget what I read about Lloyd's condition: "Patient is in severe respiratory distress. He is not good and most likely will not make it through the night." As I sat there reading that, it still didn't occur to me that he would die. I don't know, and I still don't know, whether I was in denial. Maybe I really believed he would get better in time and pull through this.

They hooked him up to a bigger breathing machine with a long hose that led up to his mouth. It kind of reminded me of a sleep apnoea machine but much bigger. The staff also had to restrain him because he kept trying to pull it off.

As his condition got worse, he grew more and more agitated. I had heard of the "death rattle," the kind of sound someone makes when they're dying, and I heard it coming from Lloyd. He was also starting to hallucinate and speaking gibberish.

When I was finally allowed back in to see him, the nurses told me that they were phoning the doctor to come in. The time had come to get Lloyd intubated. At this point, he didn't know me anymore.

I went out to tell his family what was happening and then went back to Lloyd's bedside. The doctor came very quickly but told me to leave once he was ready to do the procedure. I kept hugging Lloyd and telling him that I loved him.

"Get her out of here right now," the doctor said to the nurses.

So I gave him one last hug, told him one last "I love you," and then turned to go. But then I turned back around to Lloyd and added, "See you soon."

Then I was gone.

I went to the waiting room, lay on the couch, and just cried. My mother-in-law told me that everything would be all right. But for the first time in three days, I knew they wouldn't be.

I remember one nurse calling "Code blue" over the PA system and I knew it was Lloyd. Shortly after that, a nurse came back to talk to us. He'd had a heart attack. The intubation had exerted too much strain on his body.

"Well, what does that mean?" I asked. "Is he still here?"

"Yes, but it doesn't look good," she said. "They are working on him."

I immediately went to the payphone and called my parents. It was about 1:20 a.m. now and I told my mom that Lloyd had just suffered a heart attack. It didn't look good and they should come right away. And they needed to call the pastor.

At 1:29 a.m. on Tuesday, July 18, 2006, my husband, Lloyd Robert Ehrienfried Lee, died.

When the nurse and doctor came out to tell us, I started screaming and remember falling. Lloyd's uncle was there and caught me just as I was about to hit the floor. I screamed out some obscenities to God.

"There is no God," I screamed. "If there was, this wouldn't have happened."

"Julie, don't say that," Lloyd's uncle said. "Your faith is way too important to you."

All I responded was with "Not anymore!"

It took me a while to go back and see his body. I couldn't face it.

About five minutes later, or so it seemed, my parents came in. My pastor was there and so was Lloyd's cousin.

I next went out to the payphone and called our friends from Toronto to let them know what had happened, as they had been receiving regular updates all night. They jumped in the car and drove over right away.

I also phoned my cousin and his wife. I was still in such a state of shock that I couldn't believe I was calling people to let them know my thirty-two-year-old husband had just died.

I was continuing to shout obscenities to God. I just didn't understand how Lloyd could go through so much. Why would God would allow this to be the end result? Lloyd had fought so hard. His faith had been solid. Now I was a widow and single mother, not knowing what I was going to do next. What would I do for the rest of my life without Lloyd?

Suddenly, the horror hit me next. My sister! She didn't even know yet and she was at my house staying with the kids. Everybody was here together at the hospital and she was probably sound asleep at home.

Lloyd's cousin offered to go back to my house to be with the kids so my sister could be with me. My dad drove over and brought my sister back to the hospital.

I must have gone back in to see Lloyd's body a half-dozen times. I went with Lloyd's parents, with my parents, with my sister, with our friends from Toronto, with the pastor, and a couple times on my own. After about the third time, I became numb to it all.

We finally left the hospital at around 5:00 a.m. in my dad's truck with my parents and sister. We went back to my parents' house. There, my sister and I crawled into my parents' bed and just lay there. She wrapped her arms tight around me, but I couldn't close my eyes. When I did, all I could see was Lloyd hooked up to that stupid ventilator and how yellow he looked.

The next few hours were spent with family and friends stopping by with food and flowers. The coroner's office even called to ask me if I wanted an autopsy done. Again, I was completely offended.

"No!" I yelled. "I know how he died!"

I didn't want anyone cutting him up. In retrospect, I wish now that I'd had it done, just to know if he might have been suffering from anything else we didn't know about.

When my dad went to get the kids from our house, again the horror hit me. How on earth would I tell my five- and three-year-old that their daddy was never coming home? I sat them down on the edge of my parents' bed and explained the situation—although not in huge detail, because they wouldn't understand. I said that Daddy had been very sick and the doctors hadn't been able to make him better. Did they cry? No, they didn't. They didn't get it, not even Delaney, and she was both the oldest and her daddy's girl.

But at five and three, of course they wouldn't understand. All they knew was that something felt different.

My dad told me that it was time to go to the funeral home and make arrangements. I dreaded this part. Needless to say, a lot of the decisions were left up to my dad. I just went along because I had to. He chose the cards to hand out at the service and I wrote the obituary for the paper.

My aunt called one morning and told my mom that she hadn't been able to sleep the night before, so she'd prayed for God to give her some comfort. She had opened her Bible to this scripture:

> The righteous perish, and no one takes it to heart; the devout are taken away, and no one understands that the righteous are taken away to be spared from evil. Those who walk uprightly enter into peace; they find rest as they lie in death. (Isaiah 57:1–2 NIV)

So that's the verse I had printed on the cards that my dad picked out for the service.

I chose not to have Lloyd's service for a couple of weeks. Although I said it was to allow time for people to be notified who lived out of town, I must admit that it was more for me. I wasn't ready for the service yet. After the service would come the cemetery, and then it would all seem so final. It all felt so surreal, like I was there preparing for it all but it wasn't me.

Lloyd's service was held on Saturday, July 29. It was a celebration of life at our church. My mother-in-law took me out a few days before to buy an outfit for the occasion, something which I didn't want to do. My doctor had prescribed me Lorazepam because I wasn't sleeping or eating. I was very distraught.

The service was beautiful. I had chosen to display pictures by category: Lloyd the father, Lloyd the husband, Lloyd the son, Lloyd the friend. It looked so good. I had also picked three songs to play at different parts of the service: "When I Get Where I'm Going" by Brad Paisley and Dolly Parton, "Sandy's Song" by Dolly Parton, and "Praise You in This Storm" by Casting Crowns.

Although I had taken a step back in my faith, love, and trust for God, I knew that He was still in control. He was still there for me, which is why I chose "Praise You in This Storm." The lyrics suited me perfectly. I was going through this tremendous storm, but God never left my side, no matter what. He heard my cries.

The skies thundered and rained during the service while the song played. I couldn't believe it. It was quite beautiful, like God was speaking and that He knew my pain and was listening.

And for a brief moment I felt at peace, knowing without a shadow of doubt that Lloyd was in heaven at home with Jesus.

Eleven

The next few weeks and months were very difficult. Very stressful. I had to sell my house and the kids and I moved in with my parents. I sold it mostly because I couldn't go back there to live.

I did go back and clean up the blood around the toilet, though. And when the time came to pack Lloyd's things, I thought it was something I had to do, something only I should do. But I just went into the closet and smelled all his clothes and fell to the floor holding onto them. My cousin's wife, who was there with me, came in and took the clothes from my arms. She hugged me and then took over. I couldn't do it. I couldn't bear to put his clothes in a box.

Selling my house was very hard, especially because just before Lloyd went into the hospital we had been talking about how much we loved our house. It had felt complete. The feeling of completeness was now gone and I felt a big hole in my heart.

I continued to lay in bed day after day, until my dad came in and made me get up, made me get dressed and eat. He basically kicked my butt and told me to start looking after my kids, because they needed me. I was in a place where I didn't care what happened to me. I didn't care whether my parents were raising my kids or not. I loved my kids more than anything, but I didn't care to raise them. I was a complete mess.

What's the point? I thought. *I can't do this alone. I can't live without Lloyd.*

Oh, but did I ever find out that I was never alone! God gave me a great family and the ability to see it eventually. I wasn't alone and could feel His presence even at my lowest points.

When at my lowest, I literally fall to my knees, or onto a piece of furniture, and cry, "God, my God, where are You? Why have You left me?" At times I have felt so alone. I've felt betrayed, like God has forsaken me. These thoughts and feelings go through my mind every day.

Looking back, though, I realize that God was more present and real to me than ever. And like the famous poem says, those are the times when I look back and see only one set of footprints in the sand. Because God was carrying me!

I felt like I was walking directly towards the storm. Then I entered it head-on. I kept hearing God's words tell me to trust Him. While walking in the middle of the storm, all I could hear was God telling me over and over, "Trust in Me. Close your eyes and walk through the storm—not around it but through it. Trust Me." That seemed to be the common theme during those five months. Trust in Him. Believe. Have faith. Trust in the unknown. Walk into the unknown. Let Him guide you.

For some reason, I have to walk through the storm, not around it. There are things on the other side of the storm that are unknown to me, but I believe they are good.

For now, though, God's will is for me to walk through the storm. To get what is on the other side, I need to experience this. I will continue to praise Him through it.

My dad helped me get back on my feet in the days and weeks after Lloyd's death, especially when I cursed God and flat-out hated Him for allowing this to happen. My dad would call our pastor to come talk to me. He persevered until I was finally able to see that this wasn't God's fault. That doesn't mean I wasn't still mad, or that I stopped asking why. I must have asked why every day for the next five years.

One day I was at the store with my mom. We had gone our separate ways and agreed to meet back at a certain time. I stood in the aisle looking at a diet pill I had been on for a month after gaining some weight. I grabbed it off the shelf and read the label, wondering whether I wanted to continue taking it.

Suddenly, a woman came up to me and started asking me questions about the pill. I explained that I had only taken it for a month and hadn't actually lost any weight yet. That said, I had noticed that I now had more energy.

We had stood in the aisle talking for about ten minutes about weight and how much harder it was to lose weight when a person is older, especially considering all the different diets out there nowadays. Then the conversation turned to the subject of support groups.

"Is your husband supportive of your diets?" she asked.

I didn't know what to say. Knowing I would never see this woman again, I could just lie. Or should I tell her the truth?

I decided to be honest and tell her that my husband had passed away in July. She was so sympathetic and supportive that I thought she was going to cry. She then leaned over, gave me a big hug, and told me how sorry she was.

We proceeded to talk about faith and God and how important it is to have those things and believe that God works in our lives for the better, even though we don't necessarily think so at the time. We just need to continue trusting in God, believing that He will bring us through not only the good times but the bad ones. I told her that my family and faith had helped get me through so far. She then asked whether she could pray for me and put me on the prayer list in her church. I agreed without asking what church she belonged to. I didn't think it mattered.

"You know, I believe I was meant to meet you today," she said. "God places certain people in your life at certain times and I think this is one of those times."

How cool this was! She was right. She had given me so much comfort despite being a total stranger.

After asking about my children, she told me that she would pray for me. She then gave me her name, and I gave her mine. We hugged one more time and said goodbye.

I got was the weirdest feeling, almost like she was an angel for having known exactly what to say. She was just an awesome woman.

I was late meeting my mom, but we paid for our purchases together and walked out the door. That's when I saw the woman again. She followed me and my mom to my car, where we spoke a second time. I said goodbye once more and told her how nice it had been to meet her.

Then she vanished. My mom and I didn't even see where she went.

Is it possible that God sent her to me? Do I believe that? Yes, I do! Obviously, I needed some encouragement at that point in time. Am I still on those diet pills? No, I'm not! It's funny how God works in our lives. He knows what we need and when we need it.

At times I still get angry with God, but I know He can handle it. I went to grief counselling faithfully for five years after Lloyd's death. I've also been given gifts from God, including beautiful dreams about Lloyd. I know where he is, that he's okay and with Jesus, and that one day I will see him again.

Where am I now? How have the intervening years been for me? Well, I'm in a really good place in my walk with God. I've had so many changes in my life, some good, some bad. I haven't always been happy and I haven't always made the wisest choices. Lloyd's death really messed me up, but instead of dwelling on mistakes and the past I have learned to move forward and focus on what God wants for the lives of me and my children. I am meant to take one day at a time.

First and foremost, I am a mom. That's my number one priority. My girls are everything to me and I'm so glad to have them. God's grace and mercy have brought me out of the depths of despair—more than once, I may add. God is faithful, just, and ready to forgive us. My storm was hard. It was intense! It still is, most of the time, but my journey gets a little easier day by day. My life from now on is up to God and His decisions, as long as I'm willing to walk through this life and journey with Him.

Sometimes I get stuck on the why because my life has changed so much. Things aren't the same now and our family has a void. Why did this happen, and why did it have to happen now and not when the kids were older? At least they would have had more time with him. They would remember him. Why did God allow him to get sick in the first place?

I tried so hard to figure it all out. Once I stopped trying, I was more at peace. There was nothing I could do about any of it. Lloyd was gone. He wasn't coming back.

Isaiah 40:31 says, *"[B]ut those who hope in the Lord will renew their strength. They will soar on wings like eagles; they will run and not grow weary, they will walk and not be faint"* (NIV). I've learned to move on, and God has given me the strength and courage to do that. I've always said that when I get to heaven, the first thing I am going to ask Jesus is why. But I have a feeling that I'll be a little distracted when I get there and it won't matter.

A friend of mine once said to me, "Lloyd is not about his death. He is so much more than that." So over the years I've tried to change my focus from my grief and moving on to who he was and the legacy he left. I do this instead of dwelling on the doom and gloom of his sickness and death. Lloyd was an amazing person. He was my best friend, an awesome husband, an amazing father, and the kindest man you could ever meet. He would have done anything for anybody. He loved life, and

I believe he lived it to the fullest. The biggest legacy he left is his two daughters, and I see him in both girls. He taught me how to be kind and work hard. He taught me how to love without worrying about getting hurt. He loved and supported his family.

I would like to think that God has let him look in on the girls and me at special times, like the first time I donated blood in his honour, or my very first day at my new job after not working for nine years, or Delaney's horseback riding competition or Ella playing the piano.

It's taken me so many years to complete this book. When I started writing it, Lloyd was still alive. I began it after we got back from the Mayo Clinic, when he was doing well. My intentions were to finish the manuscript so he could read it. I started typing it up on our old school computer. He saw it at one point, but I quickly told him not to read it. It was meant to be a surprise.

Sadly, he didn't get the chance to read it.

For the first five years after he died, I wasn't thinking straight. I wasn't in a good headspace. I had fallen away from the Lord. I felt lost without Lloyd and didn't know what I was doing as a single mom. Even though I had tons of help from my parents and sister and brother-in-law, I felt alone. I always felt the hole in my heart from Lloyd not being there. I felt broken. I made so many mistakes and hurt so many people along the way.

But I've been healing, and I've come to realize that I am not defined by my mistakes.

Yes, those first five years were very hard. I was trying to figure things out, live without him, and be a good mother to a normal family. God has changed me, though. He changed who I am. He has shown me so much in regards to Lloyd's death. I'm not sad all the time anymore. Beauty has definitely come out of ashes.

I still miss Lloyd every day. That hasn't changed! I've been trying to raise my kids in a way that would honour him and make him proud. It hasn't always been easy. In fact, most often it has been very hard. My kids and I have faced many challenges. Delaney and Ella are now grown up and don't remember their dad. But they have heard many stories about him, and because Lloyd and I were always so close to my parents, my mom and dad talk about him and their time together.

As long as I'm still living, the stories of Lloyd will never end. My girls are gifts, and without them I wouldn't have this amazing life.

I've mentioned trying to be a normal family, but we are anything but normal. I couldn't even tell you how abnormal we are. But what is normal? How do you define normal? Normal sounds boring anyway. It's been hard having to move forward and learn to live without Lloyd, but we do it. Why should we strive to be a normal family when we aren't? My girls and I are very close. We are journeying through this life together. It's beautiful, it's crazy, it's sad, it's confusing, and it's perfectly imperfect. I think Lloyd would be proud!

As I end this part of my story, I'm proud to say that I knew this man I could call my husband and best friend. I'm proud to have his children and be the mother of these two beautiful girls. Knowing what I know now, I wouldn't change a thing. I had fourteen amazing years with this man, and his sickness, death, and everything I went through—and all my mistakes over the years—have made me the strong, independent, believing, God-fearing woman I am. Lloyd was my first love, the love of my life, and I had the honour of falling in love with my soulmate. Some people don't even get the privilege to fall in love once! I've had to learn to live without that, without him. Life has had to look different for us. It's had to change.

Lloyd is gone, but his memory remains alive forever. He is safe with Jesus walking the streets of gold. That I know! And he will be waiting with arms wide open to meet us again.

I love you, Lloyd. Until we meet again…

Photos

Lloyd at our wedding (1996).

Lloyd and me at our wedding (1996).

Lloyd, Delaney, Ella, and me (2004).
Delaney is three and Ella is one.

Gospel groups hit high note for Courtice man

Lloyd Lee, shown here with wife Julie and daughters Delaney and Ella, has to travel to the United States for treatment for a rare blood disease.

A newspaper article reporting on our church's fundraiser (2005). Delaney is four and Ella is two.

Lloyd hunting at the hunting camp, his happy place (2005).

91

My mom and dad, along with Delaney and Ella at my parents' cottage after Lloyd died. The girls spent a lot of time with my parents and the cottage was one of their favourite places (2009).

My mom and dad, along with Delaney and Ella, attending Delaney's Grade Eight graduation (2014).

My mom and dad and Ella going to Ella's Grade Eight graduation (2016).

Delaney, Ella, and me at Christmas (2023).

Delaney, Ella, and me (2024).